Finding Your Roar

Dionne Griffin McGee

Finding Your Roar by Dionne Griffin McGee

Published by DG McGee Enterprises, LLC

www.DGMcGee.com

© 2019 Dionne Griffin McGee

All rights reserved. No portion of this book may be reproduced in any form without permission from the publisher, except as permitted by U.S. copyright law. For permissions and general information, contact: info@dgmcgee.com

Cover by DW Design Pro

Attribution -ShareAlike 3.0 Unported (CC BY-SA 3.0) for checkbox icon used under public license. This non-commercial work has not been adapted and license is available at:
https://creativecommons.org/licenses/by-sa/3.0/

PMP® is a registered trademark of the Project Management Institute. CSM® is a registered trademark of Scrum Alliance, Inc. Candy Crush™ is a trademark of King. Microsoft® Excel is a trademark of Microsoft Corporation or King. Facebook™ is a trademark of Facebook, Inc. LinkedIn® is a registered trademark of LinkedIn Corporation. Walmart® is a registered trademark. Dress for Success℠ is a service mark of Dress for Success Worldwide Corporation. This book is neither affiliated with, nor authorized, sponsored, nor approved by these trademark holders.

This work comprises careful records of events, locales, and conversations. However, some names, details, and identifying characteristics are changed to protect the privacy of individuals, and to comply with corporate policy. All views expressed in this work are my own to demonstrate relevant points.

DEDICATION

I dedicate this book to those three strong women who raised me—my mother Velma, my grandmother Helen, and my Aunt Catherine. You showed me what faith in God, hard work, and strength of a woman look like. Likewise, my paternal grandmother, Carrie, taught me tenacity, problem-solving, and thinking outside the box. This is how I became a lion in the jungle versus a lion in the zoo. Without them, I wouldn't have seen the strength of a real woman. I strive daily to make them proud, as I know that they have prayed a multitude of prayers on my behalf.

CONTENTS

	Preface	1
1	Leaving the Discomfort of Comfort	7
2	A New Role	13
3	Lions in the Jungle Vs. Lions in the Zoo	25
4	The Toxic Team Unites	61
5	The Lonely Walk	69
_	Afterward	81
_	Discussion Questions	89

ACKNOWLEDGMENTS

I'd like to extend thanks to my family—my husband Corey for pushing me to take thorough notes, since I couldn't get the support that I needed from HR. Those notes turned into this book.

To my daughter Mel and son CJ for loving me just the same, even though I felt like a horrible mom some days and couldn't make all of their events, trying to climb this so-called corporate ladder.

To my Dad, Larry, and sister Alexandria for their listening ears and support.

To Rich, for believing in me and knowing we couldn't have accomplished all that we did without each other.

To Tom, thank you for your understanding and objectivity.

To all of my colleagues who didn't pass judgment based on what they heard.

To my corporate mentor, Willete for allowing me to vent as needed and giving me the best advice that she had.

To Sheila and Eduardo, thank you for being great colleagues and allowing there to be some balance with dedicated employees.

To my former employee and now editor, Robin. I appreciate you more than you know and thank you for actually coming to work and being professional. Robin you are the cream of the crop. I now understand why we really met. It wasn't the job—it was this project and more to come. Thank you for being the true editor that you are. We both survived the zoo. You witnessed this drama with your own eyes. You've worked with me for years and you know how valid but sad this situation was. However, it gave us the opportunity to work together again, like old times.

To every leader across the globe who has experienced the loneliness of leadership—don't dim your light to make others feel comfortable. Be the leader, the lion in the jungle that you truly are. Leaders lead, regardless. As lions in the jungle we control our own destiny. We hunt and get our own food; lions in the zoo wait for others to feed them. Those without drive won't get you and that's perfectly fine. They are just the wrong group of people to lead. Remember, you can't lead people who don't want to be led. Stagnation is a disease and we are immune. Success is what you make it.

Last, but not least. I thank God for keeping me in the right frame of mind. When things got rough, He told me not to move. He reminded me that there was a purpose behind the pain and a lesson to be learned. I understand that gender biases are still real in the corporate space and he allowed me to go through it to set some other people free.

I've learned that sometimes people won't like you just because. Sometimes I feel that my spirit upsets others' demons. Nevertheless, the lion still lives. I shall live and help others grow as leaders in corporate America, in their homes, in their businesses, and in life. Life is tough, but we never lose. We always win, because there's a lesson in it. It's up to us what we do with the lesson. I will continue to speak, coach, and consult others to let their lights shine by any means necessary.

PREFACE

THE LION INSIDE

Did you sense as a kid that there was a leader—a lion inside of you? That you were different from the status quo? A person who could help change the world? To coach, mold, and guide others to the next level? Early on, I knew that the lion was there, ready to roar, ready to stand fast, ready to lead.

There's a reason the lion is iconic across cultures throughout the world. It is represented in mottos and crests, art and literature. It is both feared and revered. It is largely misunderstood as well—lions are affectionate and playful; they meow and purr as well as roar, and they are cooperative and community-minded. The lion is surprisingly complex. And, it is rightly equated with leadership, being courageous, cunning, tough, tenacious, and able to shift seamlessly from teamship to solo action as needed.

From childhood, I felt that I could be an asset to an awesome company. I knew I was a lion—even if the lion was packaged as a petite, African-American female.

WHY LISTEN TO ME?

So why should you listen to me? Am I smarter than you? Tougher than you? More privileged than you? Probably not. What I am is aware of my value as an individual and as a leader. Aware of the challenges I've faced and will continue to encounter. I am a businesswoman, a wife and mother, a mentor, a motivational speaker, and a woman of faith. I've learned to use my voice. I've learned to speak up and speak out.

Helping people discover and awaken their own strengths is my privilege and my passion. I firmly believe that you can overcome your circumstances to achieve success. I know, because I overcame mine.

Growing up in a broken home, being raised by my mother, grandmother, and aunt, I saw the daily struggles of a woman. I saw what life looked like when you give so much of yourself to others that you lose the very essence of who you are. I saw the early morning rise, the long work hours. This was before remote work was a thing. I witnessed the ugliness of laundry, dishes before there were automatic dishwashers. Cooking home-cooked meals from scratch, no box recipes, without a microwave. An era where parents helped with homework and teachers could actually pop the kids if they were out of line. Cleaning our homes, before we had cleaning ladies. There just weren't enough hours in a day, and the effort of good parenting was often unappreciated.

As I grew up with these amazing role models, my goal was to take all the strength and courage that I now had because of these women and change the world. I wanted to call time out for women being "hidden figures."

Why do we have to be behind the scenes, I wondered? Why can't we share our light with the world? That became my mission—to be that light that the world needed. What I found on this journey of making my mark in life was that sometimes our light can shine so bright that it awakens the darkness within others and leads us into conflict. Even when we are doing the right thing. Even if it's within the workplace.

But working my way up the corporate ladder was what I had resolved to do—because I saw the struggle of three strong women. To climb this ladder, I needed to leave my hometown and the women who had lifted me to that first rung. The ladder that I saw only on television seemed to be my way out of humble beginnings. The climb was more difficult than some would have you believe.

As you climb, you encounter dangers, unexpected things that try to loosen your grip, test your footing, and extinguish that light you bear. You will encounter rooms that you don't want to be in. Colleagues who make it their goal to dim your light. You will work so hard, and sometimes you will slip. But hang tightly to your dream, and protect that light you carry within you. I too had setbacks. But I'm a firm believer that our current circumstances don't determine our future.

Having my daughter months after my high school graduation made my college hopes look dismal. My corporate dreams began to look faded. My hopes of leaving my humble beginnings seemed unreachable. For a time, I believe these challenges allowed me to have the wrong people in my circle. People who didn't have any hopes or dreams of their own. Misery loves company and I was miserable for a bit.

I felt my light dimming, but the memory of what those three strong women taught me helped me regain my footing. I had to shake off all the excuses and the people who came along with them and to remember my original dream.

I moved to Raleigh to prepare a life for me and my daughter. My support system was strong. I allowed my daughter to stay in my hometown for one year as I prepared a home for us and as I began to learn my way around a city that was foreign to me. I was just 1.5 hours from my family if needed, but at times it seemed as if I were weary months away.

Through trials and tribulations, we made it. I remember times when I'd paid all our bills and we had $20 left until the next paycheck. But we weren't homeless nor hungry. I still worked my dream because of the strength that lived in me. I went on to get my associate's degree. That degree grew to a bachelor's degree. From there, I earned a Project Management Professional® (PMP) certification, and finally a SCRUMMaster® (CSM) certification. Sometimes naps stood in for nights of sleep as I pursued each goal—I was determined that we would never have to live paycheck to paycheck again. I sometimes look back and wonder how this all happened, but it was nothing short of my faith in God, perseverance, and answers to the prayers that the three strong women had prayed over me.

Today, my husband and I have two beautiful children, and we thank God for them daily. We've imparted to our children the importance of a relationship with God, education, and a good work ethic. These are keys to success, and our children seem to be thriving with these values.

THE ROLLER COASTER RIDE THAT IS WORK LIFE, AND WHY WE DON'T TALK ABOUT IT

Building my own career has been an amazing journey—more of a roller coaster ride, really. I spent 13 years in the telecom industry, growing steadily toward a career in project management. Eventually, I made the shift to the utility industry, where I labored another eight years in various project management roles. This industry afforded me a number of opportunities (and headaches). I started this role as a consultant and was soon asked to join the company. In time, I was promoted to manager and then senior manager.

The proposal management role was also the job that introduced me to challenges such as I'd never encountered nor imagined. It pushed me to my limits in many, many ways. It opened my eyes to the types of workplace challenges we tend to shove under the table. We avoid the unpleasant truths that some teams really are toxic, that Human Resources really can be resourceless, and that sometimes our own leaders are ineffective or indifferent and some just don't have the emotional intelligence to grasp the struggle of a female leader.

These truths are some of the scariest aspects of our work. They are also where the story gets interesting, friends. This is where I share with you my own roller coaster ride through professional pitfalls that may make you want to close your eyes. But this is where perseverance enters. It's where I speak up and speak out.

And it's where I hope that I can encourage and inspire you through your own trials—to find that lion inside.

Note: Discussion questions appear at the end of the book to encourage your own thoughts and to foster discussion within workshops and groups.

Dionne Griffin McGee

1 LEAVING THE DISCOMFORT OF COMFORT

Once they reach adulthood, young male lions leave the comfort of their pride and strike out on their own, where they hone their skills before seeking a new pride to claim as their own. This is a solitary and dangerous time for the young adult lions, a proving time.

One of the greatest challenges you may face in your career is comfort—or complacency. Whatever we call it, the status quo may be less "quo" than you imagine. Lions must be ready to run with the current reality.

SOMETIMES, RIGHT THINGS HAPPEN IN UNEXPECTED WAYS

During my stint in the telecom industry, I was eventually promoted to a remote position as an Implementation Project Manager. My perseverance and effort had paid off in a position that I could enjoy and excel in. I had the comfort that can come with the status quo, but I was also restless and weary. I needed more time for family and professional growth, but my hectic schedule allowed little time for them.

I was in that mindset when a colleague and I ended a conference call about 15 minutes before our weekly team meeting. I jumped from the conference call to the 11 am team meeting call, to be told that the colleague from the first meeting hadn't joined because she had a "family emergency." Well I knew that wasn't true because she and I had just ended a conversation.

That was the tipoff. I knew it was lay-off day. Guess who else got the call shortly after?

My manager Paula called to advise me that she hated to make the call, and as soon as she saw my name on the lay-off list three days prior, she did all that she could to stop it.

She shared that she hadn't eaten in days and had been subsisting on a diet of ibuprofen instead. Over the course of our conversation, rather than her consoling me, I was consoling her. Eventually, she said "Wait, you are taking this far too well. What's going on? "

Laughing, I reassured her, "Don't worry." Paula didn't know that this setback was in fact an answered prayer. Because she was a fellow Christian, I knew that I could share with Paula my SFGTD can. In my "Something for God to Do" can, I explained, I would place mountain-top prayers that I had verbally prayed to God; I would then write the request on a sticky note with the date and time. I next thanked God for fixing my situation, because I knew that these prayers were nowhere within my power or strength to resolve.

Just seven days prior to this call from my manager, the request that I placed in my SFGTD can was…

God, I thank you for all that you have done. But I am tired. I need a break, I need to spend more time with my family, I need to increase my income, and I need to study diligently for my Project Management Certification. I have the faith that you will make a way out of no way, because I can't see how this will work, but I know that you will fix it on my behalf. In your name I pray. Amen.

Just seven days later, I got the phone call that supplied me with the time I needed to spend with my family, the time I needed to study for my certification, and a nice severance that provided that increase I asked for, along with unemployment benefits. Now, do you understand why I was laughing when the layoff call came?

Be careful what you ask for because you just might get it. You may get it in a way that looks foreign, but works for your good. And be specific—God has a sense of humor. But He knows your need even better than you do.

Paula replied in relief, "Ahhhh, I get it. That is AMAZING!"

"You were worried for nothing and missed meals for no reason, because I am fine and will remain fine," I assured her.

Paula went on to say, "Dionne, the only way you won't work is if you don't want to. You are dedicated, tenacious, and passionate about all that you do and you have been an amazing asset to the team. I know far too many people for you to be unemployed. Please send me your resume and I will broadcast it to everyone I know."

"I appreciate your kind words and support, but don't move too quickly, because I want to take God up on his offer, because he did all that I asked him to and I want to take some time to enjoy every second of it."

Considering that I had been working since high school, I called it a mini-retirement. The lay-off from the company I'd spent the last 13 years with was to be expected due to resource duplication with the acquiring company, and they had a union. This was my time.

THE TEST

Therefore, I took a break from the workplace just to catch my breath, spend some time with my family, and relax. After a week of that, I went back to work.

Kidding. I began to work on my Project Management (PMP) certification and I cherished the time that was gifted to me. I placed my son on the bus in the mornings. Some mornings I had the luxury of taking him to school. I prepped meals for the week and placed all our meals in the crockpot in the morning. I then studied four-plus hours daily for my PMP certification. I took daily naps after my studies so that I would be refreshed when my son came home from school. My firefighter husband and I rotated homework duty when he was off shift.

My project management skills helped make my time at home both productive and enjoyable. My three-month reprieve would soon draw to a close, but I had made my time count, and I was ready to sit for the PMP certification test. I had taken my exam preparation book to my children's track meets, football games, road trips etc. I continued to refresh my studies and even took a PMP Boot Camp—I refused to sit for the test unprepared.

Finally, I had studied until I couldn't study any more. My husband and I went on a date night to see Kevin Hart. I told him I just needed to laugh, to get rid of all my stressors before sitting for the exam that I had scheduled for the next morning. To my surprise, no seats had been available in my area, so I drove one and a half hours the next day to take the 4-hour exam in another city.

I completed the exam in three and a half hours. As I stared at the computer screen, awaiting my results, my heart hammered wildly. This is a notoriously difficult certification to acquire, and the test is a beast. I gave all that I had for the test, and within a few moments I would know the results of my effort.

"**Calculating your results**" flashed onscreen. I was about to lose it.

Moments later, a new screen displayed "**Passed**."

I threw up my hands and declared "Thank you, Jesus" as the joyful tears began to flow down my face. I gave it all. A nearby camera in the testing facility caught a proctor's eye; he thought that I needed a pencil or some scratch paper for my formulas. I was too overcome to even talk to the proctor. I just fanned him away. I'm not an emotional person but this really hit home.

I knew what I had asked God to do and He made a way. While I had roles as a project manager, I wasn't certified and I was determined that I would be if this was what I was going to do. The time that I needed was provided and I honored the time I was allowed. I was so happy! And my family was so proud, because they knew the effort I'd made to obtain this certification.

My superpower PMP skills arrived just in time—I'd need them sorely.

Dionne Griffin McGee

2   A NEW ROLE

It seems appropriate that lions live in groups called "prides." They are the only truly social big cats, and while they are skilled hunters, they are also cooperative and adaptable to changing conditions.

NEXT STEPS

Just as I was preparing to take that test after nearly three months of preparation, my phone rang.

Paula announced, "I have a job for you."

"Really, where?" I inquired. Paula began to tell me about a project management position with a company in nearby Raleigh. Before I could say if I was interested or not, she advised me that she told the hiring manager I was interested and to call me.

I exclaimed "Really, Paula! I guess I don't have a choice now, since you went through all of this for me."

The hiring manager had previously worked for Paula as well, but left the telecom conglomerate to go to a smaller company as a manager. The hiring manager and I had never met, as she had already left when I joined Paula's team.

So, I went to the interview and interviewed well with Mary and Dan. The role involved helping to manage proposal responses in a fast-paced environment. The next day, I got a call that they wanted me to join the team. Things began to move very fast.

I had taken three months off. I was able to spend quality time with my family and breathe for a while. I had prepared for my PMP certification. I needed it for what was to come.

THE COMPANY AND THE INDUSTRY
Quite soon, I was really engrossed in my new role with this small company. I had my PMP certification behind me. I checked the box as project managers do, to denote our completion of a task or assignment. What it really means is "I did that."

The industry was a change of pace for me—a smart-grid utility company positioned in the top three within the industry. I had done my background homework. And while I was excited about the potential that I saw for my new employer's continued growth and success, I was realistic about the stats, both there and within the utility industry nationally and globally. There would be challenges beyond routine business goals.

- My new company employed nearly 4000 people nationally, of whom fewer than 10% were people of color.
- Upper-level managers and sales staff essential to my team's success were scattered across various time zones and locales, and were frequently unavailable.
- Women make up approximately 20% of the utility industry workforce, and only 11% work in managerial positions. Within the industry, females account for 8% of Board positions and 1% of CEOs.

In short, I found myself in a new industry, a new role, and a new set of challenges to meet head-on. As leaders, we enlist to take on trouble. I would not be bored.

THE DEPARTMENT MISSION
The department existed to respond to requests for proposal (RFPs) from various utilities within the U.S. and sometimes abroad. The customers themselves set the (often monstrous) deadlines, and

proposal teams like ours mobilized to respond. RFP questions are frequently quite technical and the problems to be solved are unique to each customer—proposal work requires nimbleness, clear communication with subject matter experts (SMEs) and the sales team, and careful number crunching.

Further complicating matters was that our decisionmakers were greedy in their approach—deciding to respond to nearly every RFP thrown over the fence rather than being selective about our best opportunities. That approach made for a constant, mad scramble. We averaged over 70 proposals per year, which equated to about 1.34 proposals due each week. Due dates and times varied, and RFPs came from around the country. Our proposals ranged from three hundred pages to thousands of pages. This pace would only increase as each year went by.

If you've ever had the opportunity to work on proposals, then you know they will suck the life out of you. It's a thankless job and it never stops. Proposals drop in your inbox without notice and with quick turnaround dates. Your personal plans go out the window. Non-forecasted proposals will put you in a bad head space.

I was used to working eight-hour days. That was over once I joined this organization. But I applied my philosophy that I'm going to give all that I have as I always do. Sixty-hour weeks back-to-back were becoming the norm. I remember one day in particular when I had gone into the office at 7 am and didn't leave until 11 pm. Insanity. That night I said to myself as I walked out alone, "How long can I sustain this? It's simply too much. Why is this happening?"

THE LEADERSHIP CHALLENGE

As I mentioned earlier, much of upper-level management was located out of state. Although we had frequent teleconferences and travel to our site, it could be challenging to establish true rapport with the executive team. They were as busy as we were. And they weren't in the proposal trenches.

Then, there was local management. As much as I liked my manager as a person, she wasn't the leader that we needed.

We didn't have the structure, planning, leadership, nor professionalism that was required for her role. Mary would come in hours after the team had arrived in the office. She would call impromptu meetings that would last for hours. These habits put us behind on our daily activities.

Moreover, she cursed like a sailor to team members and other colleagues. At times, her language became quite abusive, particularly to my male colleague, Eddy. Eddy was a non-confrontational sort, and he was understandably distressed. So much so that he came to my office to complain on a regular basis. I finally told him I couldn't take it anymore.

"Confront her, I advised. She only does it because you allow her to do so. My mom has always told me that when people lose their minds you have to correct them immediately."

I felt so bad for Eddy, but it wasn't my place to speak for him, because she would lose even more respect for him if a female had to speak on his behalf. Eddy finally quit before he would confront her.

Mary tried to talk to me one day as she talked to others. I simply went into her office and closed the door. She joked, "Uh oh! We're about to have a coming to Jesus moment." I responded "Yes we are." I advised her that "I am a professional; I expect to be treated with respect. I will respect you and in turn you will respect me. Otherwise, I will give you this laptop back so fast it will make your head spin." She apologized and we moved on. Six months later, I had to do the same thing.

HUMAN RESOURCES

Mary had shrewdly made buddies within Human Resources. While Tony and Linda from HR were very aware of her lack of professionalism, they did nothing.

Over time, it became increasingly apparent that HR was ill equipped to deal with the challenges our team posed. Exasperated, I christened them "H aren't."

THE TEAM

When I came onboard, our team of eight boasted three project managers. I was the only one certified on the entire team, which also included three technical writers; a production coordinator; my manager, Mary; and co-manager, Dan. The team flexed and grew over time, but the core remained.

Ah, the team. Eventually, I assigned the more colorful players these "titles:"

- The Underminer
- The Entitled
- The Grumbler
- The Excuser
- The Rookie

The Underminer

Dan, who worked alongside me as a project manager, was not PMP certified. He was a former colleague of Mary's from an earlier job, and frequently leveraged their personal connection to his advantage.

When I first met Dan, I could not help but notice his inherent laziness and a seeming sense of entitlement. He craved accolades without putting in the effort. Recognition, vacation, bonuses, titles etc. were all good, but he didn't give a crap about any of it. He'd do just enough to get by and make others believe that he was the cream of the crop. Longevity doesn't make you the cream of the crop. Leadership, dedication, passion, and drive do.

Did he have technical ability? Yes. But being technical doesn't make you a leader; it makes you an individual contributor with a specialty. He had managed to pull on the coattails of the leaders who came before him to win a leadership position.

With time, I learned that Dan excelled at Candy Crush and sabotage when he felt threatened. Game players will play their games.

The Entitled

One of the more seasoned members of the team, a tech writer, was like clockwork. Alex didn't care what was going on—he was leaving at 3 pm, regardless of whether we were in the end stages of closing out a project. Alex would work remote if it fit his schedule. If not, he wasn't going to make many changes to support the team.

Alex was closing in on retirement and had adopted the curmudgeon persona with relish. He was exceptionally knowledgeable, and he needed everyone else to know it. Tact was not in Alex's toolkit, and he frequently alienated colleagues, while making it his business to know what they were doing. He had strong opinions and expressed them freely, often second-guessing management decisions without knowing what drove those decisions.

The Grumbler

Debbie and Alex were about the same age, and Debbie's main objective was the same. She left at 4 pm daily. Like Alex, she would do the least work possible, while others stayed late or worked remote. Work seemed highly inconvenient for Debbie. Her chief responsibility was to triage a proposal when it came in and print the documents when it was time to deliver. She seemed to fill many of her remaining hours doing homework provided by the local community college and watching movies.

Debbie distinguished herself through misery. Her responses to my daily "Good mornings," ranged from "What's so good about it?" to a sullen non-response. Her negativity grew so unbearable that one of our sales reps actually requested that I ban her from his meetings. Eye rolling, door slamming, and grousing were just an average part of her day.

So, Debbie had a pie job, and if you asked her to do more than that, it would be attitude all over the place, huffing and puffing as if she were a kid in kindergarten. Remember, she was retirement aged. Was this attitude fair to the rest of us who were working 60-plus hours weekly? I couldn't help but wonder what she was doing for hours, days, and weeks where she didn't have anything to triage or print. She surely didn't step up and ask "How can I help my fellow team members?"

Because she was so miserable, I wondered why she didn't change jobs, but I realized that she was unlikely to find another position that required so little of her. People like that you have to stay away from. She was 100% toxic, through and through.

The Excuser

Harley. The carpets by her office may still be damp from the tears. A petite, attractive woman who could be quite good at her job, Harley was a prisoner to the drama of her daily life. She could never grasp what was expected of her as an adult and a professional in corporate America. It was always about what she wanted to do when she wanted to do it.

She kicked off our relationship by saying that she had a problem being on time. Her eventual solution was to move 45 minutes farther away. It was a make-believe world going on in her head. Harley had learned to trade on her southern belle persona and she had a suitcase full of excuses, usually conveyed via text:

- Traffic was evil this morning.
- There was an accident.
- I lost my phone—it was in my baby's toy chest.
- Husband has the flu. I have to take the baby to daycare. Will be in around 10 (shows up around 11).
- Anna Joy had a blowout. I'll be late for the meeting. I don't want to be a bad influence on the new people.

Harley was smart, but she couldn't get out of her own way.

The Rookie

One of our newer hires, Nikki, was surprisingly mature and professional—particularly in contrast with some of her colleagues. Nikki was quite young, but she was bright, hard-working, and showed great promise. I was pleased with Nikki's work ethic and actively sought opportunities for her to continue to grow professionally. Alas, she was just green enough to allow some colleagues to invite her into their drama.

No, I'm Not Heartless

Lest you think that I am an emotionless automaton, please let me reassure you. I've endured my share of heartaches and I have mothered children. I understand that people go through genuinely difficult seasons, and I can respond in compassion and kindness.

I also understand that mental illness can be a serious and debilitating condition that can be exacerbated by chronic workplace stress. I wholeheartedly encourage sufferers to seek help and to be forthright with HR and management about their steps to address any workplace problems. I too had to have sleeping pills prescribed by my primary care physician so that I could sleep at night, due to the stresses of the job.

That said, I am also a believer in leaving manufactured drama at home. Why add that to the stressors we already face at work? It was difficult for me to work in an environment of adults who seemed to act like children. I wondered, "Can we come into the office as professionals, can we come to be a part of a cohesive team, can we offer our skills and abilities to the company? And go home?" Was I asking too much? Was this not the norm?

Was I crazy? Remember, the three strong women who had guided me. All I know is hard work—not mediocrity.

Yet, mediocrity surrounded me. This team did just enough to get by, with not one ounce of character or integrity. How do people like this excel in life? I had to realize that not everyone has that light inside.

Changing Roles

Eventually we lost Mary to a layoff. Mary's confrontational management style, combined with the challenges of a toxic team, led to an inevitable showdown. An argument with a team member got so heated that it was reported to HR. Mary took several months' medical leave, returned for a short stint, and was laid off shortly afterwards.

With us now leaderless, Dan and I split the chief management role. Dan had been in the department before I had and had more experience. However, I was a certified PMP and now a certified Scrum Master, as I had earned another certification to help me in my role. I went along with splitting the role, as I knew that I was in a male-dominated, good ole' boy industry. However, I had no intentions to follow this Walmart®-type structure for long. I wasn't worried because I knew that I was a better fit, and I was just going to do what I knew was right.

Even though I came to the department after Dan, the company recognized my leadership skills and the fact that I was a certified project manager with a degree. I had built great relationships with my colleagues. Soon, I became not only the department manager, but was promoted to Senior Manager shortly afterwards.

As much as Dan acted like he was happy for me, I knew that he really wasn't. But I couldn't look back. Once I was able to make a difference or to make things better in the workplace, I took on the opportunity. I knew going in that most people don't care for their managers. Those in leadership have a hard road to travel and at times we must walk alone. I just didn't know how alone that was.

Yes, I was bold enough to confront the issues and not just sweep them under the rug as is often accepted in the working world. Some don't want to hear the truth. I only wanted what was best for the entire team, but some people would prefer that you turn a blind eye or simply lie to them. That is not my style.

Why Am I Here?
So, I'd gotten my "reward"—I inherited a toxic team.

My team consisted of two seasoned employees who needed to retire, but couldn't. I had one lazy geek, who just wanted a nice paycheck but had no goals or ambitions. A basket-case belle who wanted everything her way and was often in tears. A millennial who had no idea of the drama she was about to step into. The employee who always wanted to work remote and was never available for training, the contractor who vanished regularly without a word. This group had 0% percent integrity or accountability.

Did I mention that the projects that we produce are multi-million-dollar accounts? In spite of the challenges that came with the toxic team, the previous year we had completed almost 70 projects under my leadership. The coming months looked to be even busier.

Being a childcare provider was not on my action item list. We had work to do.

I wanted balance for my team. Balance and not working 10–14-hour days like we had with our previous manager. I too have a family and a life outside of work, and I was well aware that they did. It was important to me to use my project management skills to ensure efficiency and to honor an eight-hour workday regularly.

I began to have conversations with my HR Representative, Rhonda. "Rhonda, there is drama at least 70% of the time in my department. I am severely allergic to drama. I've wondered why I have to deal with these types of shenanigans in the workplace. Let's come in the office, respect each other, get the work done, break bread together on occasion, and go home. Let's leave the drama, gossiping, sabotage and back biting outside of the four walls."

I also began to have conversations with myself. I began to wonder. Is it because I am an African-American female managing a team of 100% Caucasians? Is it because I am managing 50% males? Maybe because I am younger than 90% of my team? Is it because I started as a contractor and worked my way up to Senior Manager, bypassing those who used to be my peers? Is it because I'm a certified project manager who eats and sleeps project management, where our former manager was not and everything was a fire drill? Is it because I care enough to be more efficient so that we can have a proper work life?

And, why in God's name was I the only African-American female in leadership with a company of roughly four thousand people?

Is it me, I pondered? Is it my sheer existence and passion for my career rather than the job? Is it the fact that I can't be run over and handled?

I soon realized that as long as I am pleasant, fair, and supportive, while bringing in revenue for the company…**what others think about me is none of my business**.

Reporting to a Vice President, my own stress level and visibility was high. I brought and continue to bring my best to the office daily. People have asked me what my role is and I simply reply "My job is to make my boss's job easy." Forget what LinkedIn says. In return I expect the same from my team.

Finally, I asked God, "Why am I here?" His response:

This is part of your journey. This is building, preparing, and creating you to be the woman that I've called you to be. I'm allowing you to deal with this trouble, as I won't put more on you than you can bear. (1 Corinthians 10:13)

Your skin is thick and I know you can handle it. Furthermore, you are not the only one dealing with this, but you are the only one strong enough to write about it. Others are suffering as well.

So, I decided to write this book for therapeutic reasons. I have come to realize that common sense isn't that common. As much as it saddens me, I realized: if I'm going through this, others are as well.

Happily, God always has a ram in the bush. Another team member was a Christian. Sheila was a technical writer who had her head screwed on straight. Down to earth, she came to work to get her job done. She was the only one that I really looked forward to seeing daily. No drama, no fluff, she had a "let's get it done" attitude. We understood each other as Christians, as mothers. We were able to pray for each other when needed. I thank God that I did have some peace in the workplace, some balance. And when Sheila left the company for greener pastures, God sent me another ram in the bush who had a major impact on this book.

My hopes are that both the leaders and the toxic employees read this book, and hopefully they will begin to see their error.

I often said, "I wish cameras could roll in my department. We would have the number one reality show. The Kardashians would've been cancelled."

But if cameras can't roll…readers can read. I did my best with those challenges, took some punches, and began a journey I had never foreseen. As a careful manager, I take notes—and the notes that I had captured over the years became invaluable. I thank God for my toxic team, as they gave me the material I needed to be an author.

3 LIONS IN THE JUNGLE VS. LIONS IN THE ZOO

Lionesses will often care for others' neglected cubs. Lions are also very communicative, licking one another and nuzzling each other in greeting. A lion's roar can be heard over five miles away.

Born leaders walk to the beat of a different drum. We know where we've come from and we know where we are headed because we are goal setters and achievers.

As a female executive, I have a special place in my heart to help women, by coaching and guiding those who I can see clearly are born leaders and have a passion to achieve their goals and excel. This is part of the reason that I volunteer for the Dress for Success℠ organization. Speaking, leading mock interviews, and reviewing resumes are capacities in which I've volunteered to help all who want to take the next step in life for the betterment of themselves and their families.

Leaders have goals and dreams that we are determined to reach no matter what. I knew that taking on this role where my former peers were now my team members would lead to some dark and dismal days. Some wouldn't like me nor the choices or decisions that I had to make as a leader.

I have thick skin, so game on. Leaders are like lions in the jungle. We plan to win, and nothing and no one will stop us. No matter what we come up against.

We won't wait for others to cater to us. Like lions in the jungle we go to get our own food. A lion in the zoo simply waits to be fed. Lions in the jungle are naturally driven with passion and desire to accomplish all that we've ever hoped for. Some days the hunt is better than others.

And I'm proud to report that in my new role, even with a toxic team, the company's Return on Investment (ROI) increased in the midst of stress and daily excuses. While in this position I can count the number of times on one hand that we worked late, with dinner included. A couple of Saturdays for a few hours, dressed in shorts. Not because the schedule wasn't in line, but because other stakeholders were late with their assignments.

I refused to miss a deadline. So, a few times a year, no big deal.

WHAT LEADERSHIP LOOKS LIKE IN THE JUNGLE
Real leaders have what we call emotional intelligence…

Working in male-dominated industries for the majority of my career, I believe that leadership can't be taught—you have to be born with it and it has to be nurtured. Some have a strong acumen in their profession, but just because you know and can do your job well does not make you a leader. We know how to lead a team through battle. Leaders know what to say and do in the workplace. We have a firm understanding of what is professional and what is unprofessional.

Sheep led by a lion can be transformed into warriors, but they first have to have the right attitude.

Topics that should not be discussed in the workplace:
- Race
- Religion
- Politics

- Age
- Medical issues
- Gossip, camouflaged as workplace frustrations
- Marital issues, and so on

Leaders look for these top-notch skills in employees

- Leadership
- Communication
- Collaboration
- Time management

MEANWHILE, BACK AT THE ZOO...

The toxic team didn't have these skills, and they certainly weren't trying to get them.

That's the difficult task of inheriting a toxic, lackadaisical team and not hiring your own or not having the support you need to gain new team members. In order to get the proper team members, that also meant that my sales organization would need to turn the faucet down in order to train new hires and get them up to speed. Otherwise, the team members who remained would have to work twelve-plus hour days in order to keep up with the work load and make all the deadlines. Turning down the fire hose would have allowed a smoother transition with a shorter training period for new hires.

That was a tough argument to win with senior management. I lobbied for a more strategic approach to targeting accounts, but it's difficult to tell a salesman not to try and get every customer. I lost the argument and zoo life continued.

DAILY LIFE WITH THE TOXIC TEAM

In my years of leadership, these are some of the excuses, lies, and lion-in-the-zoo issues that I've had to deal with.

Dan

It was game on for the controversy that was ahead of me. It was obvious that Dan had issues with my promotions and did a poor job of hiding it. He would make comments like:

"I'm glad you got the job instead of me, cause if anything goes wrong in the department all this s*** falls on you," he observed as he picked his nose. That was the precursor to the malicious acts that would follow.

Meanwhile, these were the day-to-day realities of office life with Dan.

☑

"My kid is sick—I have to leave early." No problem, but this began to occur at least once a week. I started to think that his kids were in ICU. Every week something was wrong with one of them to the point that he couldn't keep up with the lies.

☑

A package was delivered to Dan while I was out of the office, so Kim from HR opened the door to place the package on his desk for safekeeping. To her surprise, she found this large man asleep under his desk. He explained that his back was hurting, so he decided to lie down. Kim related with a laugh that he moved pretty fast anyway when she opened the door. I was out of the office, and Kim called me to report what she'd found. She was laughing so hard that she could barely speak.

☑

His love of video games far surpassed his passion for work. I remember us being in team meetings with our former manager and she would get a notification that Dan was on a particular level of Candy Crush™.

Dan's love of Candy Crush and social media was far more important than getting the job done. He felt overlooked, but seemed incapable of the above-average effort it takes to get above-average rewards. Once, one of our Directors came to town to meet with me, so that I could onboard one of our newly hired sales representatives.

I was walking them out and the Director stopped by to bid Dan goodbye. He wasn't in his office, but guess what was on his screen? Yep, Candy Crush. The Director gave me the side-eye and said "I thought you guys were busy." I replied resignedly, "We are. You see the struggles that I told you about with your own eyes."

So, the Director left him a sticky note on his monitor "You must not be too busy," before making his way to the elevator, shaking his head. Soon, Dan appeared in my office with a sheepish grin and said, "I guess I need to stop playing video games at work."

"Really!" I responded. "As the team busts their butts day in and day out. They don't need to work as hard as they are and see one of our so-called leaders playing video games. It's unprofessional. Imagine this, if I gave you an assignment to work on and you came to ask me a question, and I'm tied up with Candy Crush. How would that make you feel?"

☑

I tried over the years to help Dan grow as a leader. Some are born leaders and some need training just to cope in leadership. I tried to help so he could take it to the next level, via regular conversations, semi-annual reviews, annual reviews, etc.

One of the things I talked to Dan about was getting his Project Management Certification to boost his career. For three years, I placed the cost in my departmental budget so that Dan could get his certification. Each year, Dan ignored the opportunity. He finally decided to take a Microsoft® Excel™ class, just to say he took a class.

Lazy is an understatement. But why push for the next level if you are already reaping the benefits of doing nothing? This attitude causes career stagnation.

☑

Team members would sometimes come and tell me, "You were in a meeting, so I went to ask Dan a question, but he told me that he 'didn't give a s***,' so I waited for you to get out of your meeting."

Really?

☑

As the Senior Manager of the department, I needed a support system. I needed a right-hand woman or man. I needed a confidante to express plans and ideas with. I quickly found out that Dan wasn't that guy either. When I would share changes with him as a manager, I felt that I could do that, right? Apparently not. When I would come in the next morning, the entire team would know all that Dan and I had discussed. I expressed to Dan that as a leader you need to be able to keep conversations confidential. Dan responded with a gigantic belch and no apology.

☑

Dan was once tasked with completing essential proposal content before going out on vacation. As we neared production, I realized that we were missing a vital bond from our surety agency, part of the content for which he was responsible. Typically, it takes at least a week to get this document in our hands in order to submit it with our proposal. I was on a conference call on a Friday night, awaiting my son's pizza delivery, trying to clean up Dan's mess. I worked Saturday to get the opportunity to a place that we could still meet our deadline on Monday. I established the dream team over the weekend. We all met on Monday morning and I contacted the VP at the surety company; she said "This is a tall order, Dionne, but I'll do it for you." I had a digital version of the bond by noon.

When Dan returned from vacation, his words to me about the fiasco were "How'd you pull that off, I wanna know?" Can you please say sabotage?

☑

Dan then began to join forces with the team members, since I just wouldn't let him do this to me. Adding to gossip, bringing me gossip. He seemed to take the leader's handbook and do the opposite. I believe that his goal was to stress me out to give up my position. I had great rapport with my peers at the company, and it seemed to intimidate him. His response was to undermine me within my team.

I remember when we were co-managing, and Debbie needed to be placed on a performance plan. I set a meeting for the three of us. If you are going to reap the benefits of management, you need to be committed to it, which is why I invited Dan to the meeting. It was training for him. Once he moved to the next level, he would need to be able to handle conflict on any given day.

Right before the meeting, Dan came to me to try to get out of it. I told him I needed him there. Dan came in, took one of the chairs in the office, and moved it to a far corner. He sat in the corner the entire time. As the meeting progressed, he peeked to the left and right of his legal pad, which he held up to his face the entire time. Dan took notes in the air on his legal pad so that he didn't have to engage in the conversation.

I thought to myself, "And you want my job. You can't handle conflict." It was clear to me and to Debbie that he didn't want to be in the room. But he wanted the paycheck. This meeting was only to make Debbie better, so that the team could be better. I thought Dan was going to pass out. It was too much even to have him in the room, purely unprofessional and nowhere near readiness for leadership.

☑

I had previously spoken with Dan after my promotion about his passive aggressive comments and sabotage one morning before I had to fly out for travel.

I told him that I respected him and I needed him to respect me and my role. "The decision was made for a reason," I reminded him. "I'm not trying to manage anyone; I'm just trying to lead the team to a better place," I said.

I advised that I was over his passive-aggressive comments. The job was difficult enough and I didn't need it nor deserve it.

Once I painted the picture of who Dan really was and all that I had endured, he began to cry. I thought to myself, "You are a grown man—why are you in my office crying? No way you could you ever lead me."

He was fully aware that everything I said to him was true, and stated "I have really been an idiot."

☑

I had to speak at a conference in Denver, and I left Dan in charge in my absence. When I left, a vital project was 90% complete, which was the only reason I went. Dan was capable of closing out the 10%.

To my later surprise, he lied daily on the status reports he sent to me and in the conversations that we had, that everything was on track. When I returned, I found that he'd taken a three-day staycation in the office. He didn't do a thing, placing our project three days behind schedule.

I advised the team that we would have to work the weekend to recover and submit the proposal on time. Dan began to complain that his niece was coming to town and he hadn't planned to work over the weekend. That should have been on his mind three days prior. I had a stern conversation with Dan, basically stating that I was disappointed and so was my VP, Rick.

I requested a post mortem for the three days and how things could have been handled differently so that they would not happen again.

He was clearly upset. I stated, "You have a management title and reap all the benefits of a manager, with zero direct reports—and you don't want to manage even in my absence for three days."

I saw the sabotage that was set for me. This would be one of the largest proposals that we had yet submitted—worth some $90M. How do I know it was sabotage? Remember, Dan told me long ago once I was promoted. "If any of this s*** falls through the cracks, it's all on you." That comment came rushing to the forefront of my mind.

When I asked Dan for the post mortem, he replied "I don't know what I'm going to put on that paper." I advised him to figure it out because this could never happen again.

I'd had enough of the lies, sneakiness, back-biting and sabotage.

It took Dan until late that night to pull his data together. He thanked me the next morning, for making him do the exercise. He stated, "I now see what I could have done differently."

Really, you knew that then, but what you didn't factor in was that I had had enough, that I would engage Human Resources and the Vice President. I then forwarded his post mortem to Human Resources, as well as our Vice President, who was my boss.

One team member stated in the team meeting the following day. "We didn't have any leadership while you were gone. How do we make sure that when you travel, we have a go-to on site?" I told her "That is a great question, and I hate that you felt alone in my travels. For the future, please give me a call." The trouble was, they didn't want to squeal on Dan. Dan chimed in and said, "Can I answer that?" On my nod, he said "Dionne and I had a painful conversation and I realized that I should have done more as a manager and it won't happen again."

Even though I was traveling, I know that Dan spent three days on Facebook™ and playing Candy Crush in my absence. He ignored all of my advice and his own actions have stunted his career with the company. No one wants to follow mediocrity. When you step into leadership, it's not just the role. Leaders are also paid to handle conflict, criticism, opposition, and so much more. This is not who Dan was.

✓

Once I shared plans for reorganizing the department and hiring more employees so that we could handle the workload. Dan's attitude began to shift. My plans were to make him and Harley leaders and split the team into cross-functional teams, as we had a hiring freeze and no other options. He then began to sabotage Harley. He wore a path in the carpet from my office to his office, bearing negative comments. He watched when she came in, when she left, how much work she did, what she didn't do. He would bring it all to my office. It got so bad I began to close my office door to keep the drama out.

I finally had to ask him to keep it to himself. Why? He was intimidated once again; another female was in the running for his job. Every word (and I mean every word) that Harley said about me or anyone else he ran and told me every day. I already knew how Harley operated.

Considering our workload, I had to work with the resources I had. I had finally instructed him not to tell me another thing that someone said, unless he said it. It got so bad that Harley came to me crying, as Dan had told me things that she said about me years ago. Dan had acted as if she had just said them. Harley apologized and said that had been in the far past.

Soon the he said/she said drama began to unfold. Harley was so furious with Dan that she returned all the VHS tapes he had given her for her newborn to watch, leaving them in his chair while he was on a smoke break. She said, "why is he doing this to me? I haven't done anything to him. I think he's intimidated by me. If that's what it is then I don't want to be considered for the same role he has. Maybe he'll go back to being normal."

I explained to Dan that you control what goes into your ears. When you see gossip coming and you know that she is bad news, send her packing. Tell her that you are too busy right now to chat.

This is the kind of drama and unprofessionalism that played out daily. Dan wanted to make the drama begin. I really dislike gossipers—male or female. I don't have time for it.

☑

Ultimately, Dan was so consumed with me being his leader that he couldn't grow. It ate at him. So much so that it has stagnated his career.

Alex

It was so tempting to have a t-shirt printed up for Alex proclaiming, "I am here, bright and early to do the least amount possible!"

He seemed to feel that we should be honored that he showed up. May I just say that if you can't keep a handle on the cantankerousness, maybe it's time to cash in that portfolio or find a less stressful job. Alex had no interest in pleasantry whatsoever.

Typically, he scheduled his day to arrive quite early in the morning and leave at 2 pm. At least it reduced the amount of time he spent around humans.

☑

When our VP cancelled an expected visit, I sent out an email early that evening to advise the team they could work remote the next day if they wished. It was intended as a reward.

The next morning, I got this email from Alex:

"I'm here already. A little advance notice would be nice. I don't think the company should expect me to check email after normal business hours."

(WOW! You are so welcome.) I advised Alex that I never want our VP to show up when no one is available in our department. As soon as I was aware that he was not coming into the office, I sent the notice. However, since Alex likes to come in early, he was already in the office. All he had to do was get up and go home or just stay in the office. There wasn't a need to be nasty.

A few days later, I invited Alex into my office. I wanted to see how he was doing, if there was something going on with him, before I pursued our chat. I advised him that he was being a bit cantankerous lately, and I needed him to work on it.

He apologized for sending his email and then began to tell me that I was cantankerous.

"Oh, how so?"

"…I can't think of anything right now. Oh—how you go on and on in team meetings."

"Please explain how that is cantankerous if I am giving you project updates and the play book etc.?"

"You've been micromanaging the team for a year now," he concluded.

(Deep breath in and out.) "I know my job. When deadlines are missed and you don't communicate that you are slipping, it puts multi-million-dollar projects in jeopardy. So, I began to have 10-minute catch-up meetings to ensure everyone was clear on the tasks at hand. I learned that lesson a year ago when Dan and I were traveling and the entire team was late on assignments, didn't escalate to me, signed off and went home. This is how our meetings started. Remember?"

"But you're not fair to the team, and you give Robbie a pass."

"How so, Alex?"

"I can't think of anything right now, but I'll let you know. Debbie didn't get to leave and work remote one day."

"That's probably because she didn't come in on the previous Saturday and work like the others did."

"Okay, so how come Debbie isn't included in consultant reviews?"

"Debbie is aware why and that's none of your business. If you spent more time focusing on Alex and not others, we probably wouldn't be having this conversation. Like, when were you going to speak with me about adjusting your schedule?"

"Uggghh—Do you have a problem with it?"

"No, I don't, but some respect/conversation would have been nice ahead of time, just like you wanted my remote email to be. We work past 2 pm and emails still go out when you are not in the office."

☑

Alex had become increasingly cranky and super nosy, constantly walking past my office to hear and see who I was speaking with, so I moved to another office. He had become toxic to the team and had caused me to change my management approach. I went to speak with him about an assignment later and he was in a full-blown Facebook post. He was so engrossed bashing me on Facebook that he didn't even realize that I was standing there.

☑

This one was so intimidated by a new hire on the team. He felt that he was the best employee on the team since he was a senior writer, and so was the new hire. Well the new employee was a female and he hated her.

One day, Robbie made a happy-go-lucky comment in the team meeting. Alex took it the wrong way and lost it in the meeting.

Robbie was nearly in tears in the conference room. He bashed her so badly in the team meeting that I had to shut it down.

Everyone left the room and I stayed to talk with Robbie to make sure she was okay; she was just unclear on why Alex didn't like her because she hadn't done anything to him.

I spoke with him afterwards and told him that we are team members—better yet professional team members and we respect one another.

I explained if she had done this to him, I would have had a conversation with her instead. He didn't see it that way. He felt as if I took her side.

From that day forward, it was his mission to get at both of us. He was so intimidated by the new employee and so nosy that he began studying her profile and even searched her spouse's profile on LinkedIn® not long after. He forgot that LinkedIn can show who looks at your profile. This is stalking and could have really been ugly. Robbie's husband was not pleased at all and Robbie had to calm him down.

Before this incident, Alex used to sit on interview panels with me for new hires. Checking backgrounds and sites for an interview is one thing, but checking on the spouses was a bit much. I politely removed him from my panel. I engaged HR on this entire ordeal and they did nothing.

☑

At the beginning of the year, I had to reevaluate schedules and resources. I told Alex that he needed to move back to core business hours. He had taken it upon himself to move his own schedule from 7 am–3 pm to 6 am–2 pm. He simply started coming in earlier and earlier and leaving earlier and earlier, without talking with me. I advised that it was inappropriate behavior. He apologized and I allowed him to work the 6–2 until I had to reevaluate resources. Soon after, he reported to Human Resources that he was disabled and needed to work a special schedule because he was diabetic.

I had been blithely unaware that some 30 million Americans needed to work a special schedule because of their diabetes. Can I translate for you? This means "I want to come in when no one is here. I want to do less than all the other employees. This will allow me appropriate time to check the stock market and post to Facebook and eat my cheese sandwich. By the time things get busy at 2 pm, I'll be off work and headed home to feed my cats."

HR totally shut this down and advised that he needed to work based on the needs of the business. Finally, some help from HR.

☑

Later, he decided not to join one of the online training courses that the entire team was invited to. He simply left and went home. He advised in our Tuesday team meeting that he'd catch the recording. I replied that not all the trainings are recorded and I'd appreciate it if I can be informed in advance if you can't make a training and not after the fact.

☑

I asked Alex's help editing one of our projects. I explained that if he saw any missing responses for the project assigned to me or Dan to fill them in, because we were lacking resources due to our participation in a conference.

"That's not my job" he replied.

I advised it should have been simple items like address, fax #, phone etc. He asked "Are you giving me permission to fill it in?"

"Don't worry about it," I responded in exhaustion. "Skip anything that was flagged. We'll handle it." Everything was combative with him.

☑

One December, Alex was called for jury duty. I advised HR, and they requested that I get a copy of the summons from Alex. I asked him for his jury duty paperwork, as instructed.

Although Alex clearly knew what I was asking him for, he responded like this:

> *As I thought it would be obvious from my Friday status report, I was at jury duty on Monday—as required by state and county law. I didn't receive paperwork, so I don't even know what you're asking for—I can show you the summons.*
>
> *Or you can call the jury clerk for confirmation since you don't seem to believe I was there on Monday. I thought my Friday report made it clear that if I was not here, I'd be at jury duty and otherwise I'd be here.*

Once we clarified that I simply needed the summons as requested by HR, Alex informed me that I'm not a great communicator, the entire team agrees, and that I talk down to the team…

☑

I suggested that Alex might need some training courses to assist him in remaining professional in the workplace. He may also need to take adaptability training for when new employees join the team with fresh ideas.

Debbie

With Debbie, the sky was falling every day. I once greeted her, "Good morning, Debbie. How are you?"

"What's good about it?" she groused.

I took a beat and replied, "You're above ground, able to take nourishment, still in your right mind <maybe>, you dressed yourself, etc." Then she began to list how everything in her life is the worst. I'm thinking, "It's just a basic salutation, roll with it." Rarely have I seen such rage and negativity.

☑

Deadlines were quickly approaching and I walked into Debbie's office to see her doing math homework. I was floored. She responded, "I didn't see it being a problem since the company is paying for me to take the class, and I don't have anything to work on."

I just can't with these people. I guess taking the initiative as a professional to say that I need something to work on was too much to ask. Debbie was nearing retirement—I expected that she would have learned some workplace common sense. It wasn't fair that other people would come in on time and stay late when necessary—some working ten or more hours a day to get the job done. I took note. It meant that I needed to balance the workload and be more concerned with the internal equity in the department. That meant giving Debbie some other assignments that could help balance the workload for the entire team.

Boy oh boy, she hated me for that. Her pie job was gone, and I was actually asking her to do some work. Unheard of.

She asked in January if she could start coming in at 7 am and leaving at 3 pm. I told her that I didn't see that as being a problem. However, it depended on the needs of the business. Strangely, she kept her regular schedule for months, working until 4 pm. I decided that she must have changed her mind. Several months later, I sought her out to work on a project a little after three and she was gone. When I questioned her about it, she responded "Remember, you said I can start leaving at three."

"Yes, I remember, but that was six months ago and you didn't change your schedule. A follow-up conversation would have been nice, to say per our conversation earlier this year, 'I plan to start leaving at three starting next week.'"

Not long afterwards, we had a critical sales meeting at 4 pm that could be joined onsite or virtually. Guess who wasn't a part of the meeting? When I mentioned it, her response was, "I get off at 3 pm."

I was really done. I advised, "Remember the part of our conversation where I stated 'based on the needs of the business?' You could have joined remotely." This was a project kickoff call, where we needed all stakeholders on the call, especially those from the proposal department. One minor mistake could put the project in jeopardy and cost the company millions. Therefore, I asked her to return to her regular schedule, leaving at 4 pm.

She was pissed, but that was her natural state. I believe she was pissed off just because she woke up.

☑

I recall once asking her to work on a project that my VP called about at the last minute. Everyone else on the team was tied up on another project and Debbie had availability.

He called at 3:45. At this time, she was leaving at 4 pm daily. I asked her to work on this as it was an urgent request from my VP. She had a tantrum in my office, twisting and turning in the chair as if she were a toddler. She advised that she had to leave at 4 pm and this was going to take at least an hour. In reality, it took her 30 minutes to complete the request, racking up 15 minutes of overtime. A week later, she asked if she could work an hour of overtime to make up time for going to an appointment.

I brought the previous incident to her remembrance. It seemed clear that as long as her needs were met and not the needs of the business, it didn't matter. I told her that Rick, our VP, said thank you for your support and staying a little late last week. "Tell him to keep his thank you and show me the money if he is so thankful," she declared. She was so upset she went to HR, and they told her as a manager I had the right to set the schedules for the needs of the business.

☑

Later, we had to move to a cube farm on another floor of the building. Debbie was unable to acquire an office, and her cube was in the walkway of a high-traffic area near the printer. She advised us that the power didn't work in her cubicle, and she needed to move. I had maintenance come and fix the issue. Then she complained that her nerves were bad and the printer scared her, stating that she took medication for that. Realistically, Debbie had a specific cube in mind, away from the traffic, where no one could see that she wasn't working.

☑

Debbie ended up having to go on a performance improvement plan (PIP). Every time I asked her to do something, she responded with an excuse as to why she couldn't do it, or she would exaggerate the amount of time it would take to get it done. HR Rhonda came over to chat with her, and she was extremely rude to Rhonda as well.

Rhonda dropped by my desk with an "OMGeeee, you have to put up with that daily?"

I soon learned Debbie math. If I needed something completed in one day, she'd say it would take at least three. What I really wanted to say was "Please subtract the time it takes to chat with your husband online, the time that it takes to watch online movies, and the time it takes to complete your homework."

☑

Debbie was so toxic she sucked the air out of the very room she was in. The team was once working on a large account, and a sales representative flew in from Canada. I was having the entire team support the project. I soon received a call from the sales rep, Connor, saying "I really appreciate the support from you and your team, Dionne. But whatever you do, don't have Debbie in the room. I don't even understand why she is here. She can come but give her something else to do in a cubicle; she can't be in the room. I refuse to work with her."

I was like "WOW! So, I'm not crazy or insensitive; she's a mess."

☑

I've never met a more miserable person in my life. I recall preparing for a team meeting and messaging Debbie to print a document for the meeting.

When I headed upstairs for our meeting, I went by her office to get the document, but she had already left for the meeting. I decided that she must have taken the document with her, since she didn't communicate which printer to get it from. When I reached the meeting, she didn't have the document. Since I had to lead the meeting, I asked her if she could please retrieve it. She huffed, got up, and opened the door so hard that it slammed against the wall. I asked "Debbie, are you okay?"

"Yeah, yeah I'm fine."

This wasn't volunteer work. If Debbie had communicated to me where the document was, I would have picked it up from the printer, but she hadn't even acknowledged my earlier message at all.

Following a rather spectacular tantrum during another team meeting, Debbie waited a few hours, and came quietly into my office. "Do you have a minute?"

"Sure I do, what's up?"

"I wanted to let you know that I applied for another position." (I wanted to do a little victory dance, but I refrained.)

Debbie advised that she applied for a job as a Data Analyst in Marshall's organization. "Good for you, Debbie. I hope it works out for you; if I can do anything to help, please let me know."

"I apologize for my attitude earlier; I don't know what got into me." (Ummhmmm.)

She got the position, and this is the email that she sent out to a mass distro as her farewell. Remember—she was not leaving the company—just the department:

> *Hi! And Bye!*
>
> *Ummmm…WHAT…..?!?!?!?*
>
> *Ch ch ch changes, right? Here's the lowdown on mine, as unquestionably none of you is aware. I'm leaving the proposal team to take another position at the company.*
>
> *That sucks for you. Don't call me, 'cause I can't help you. (I wanted to put that out there, pronto).*
>
> *I am no longer your source for anything proposal related. For now, my duties are being split until they find my replacement (good luck with that). You'll have to contact Dan for whatever you need till then.*
>
> *I'll end my farewell with a quote from Ace Ventura— "If I'm not back in five minutes, just wait longer." That's life, people.*
>
> *To repeat, you really HAVE to call Dan for help, cause I'm outie.*
>
> *Toodles!*

I couldn't help but laugh. HR had allowed this type of unprofessionalism to transfer to another department.

Her email went viral throughout the company. Several people sent me congratulations that the "bat (X7%S) crazy" one was gone.

Harley

Harley was now a critical part of our fast-paced, high-octane and high-visibility team. Our department was a key factor in the Sales Team making their numbers. But I began to notice odd behaviors with Harley. I recalled something our previous manager had shared; Harley acted normal to get the job, then shifted into her alter ego once she was hired.

I have watched a ton of "Lifetime Movies" in my lifetime. When I came across this individual, I immediately recognized the character type. Over time, it became apparent that Harley had several dysfunctional relationships in her life. What stood out over and over was her determination to have her way. She was adept at manipulating people and circumstances to her favor. She could never grasp what was expected of her as an adult professional in corporate America. It was always what she wanted to do, when she wanted to do it. Forget about the needs of the business or her team members.

As long as she was able to connive and manipulate people to believe that she was this nice, sweet, hardworking southern belle, she was fine. But once people got close enough, they realized that she was the devil in Cracker Barrel attire. And that put Harley on high alert.

I also now understand some problems reported with her manager on her previous job. Reportedly, she made the statement "Yeah, I took care of that" when her old manager started questioning her. What I now believe after having to manage her myself, was that her previous manager was holding her accountable and she didn't like it.

Why? Because she lived in an unrealistic world. She didn't like to be managed, and she wanted to be free to do things her own way. Recall that she started off our relationship by telling me that she had a problem being on time. Really? (Leading to another pointless series of conversations with HR Rhonda.)

In spite of her unrealistic perceptions, she was good at what she did when she could just focus on the job, but her personal issues consumed her; gossiping and back-biting consumed her.

☑

The team and I were faced with an intense, non-stop workload, and the faucet just would not turn off. Deadlines stared me in the face every day. I managed as many as thirteen projects simultaneously, and there was no end in sight for the department.

It was nothing for me to work 10–12-hour days and more. I burned myself out.

I spoke frankly with my VP Rick about our need to reevaluate our approach to proposals. Finally, we agreed on a process to focus more on key proposals and no-bid others. We decided to split the department into two teams with two team leaders. One team would handle quick-turnaround projects and the other would focus on the more substantive ones. In theory, this was progress, but I needed two team leaders with the skill and commitment to get the job done.

Writers as a lot are introverts, and they are not always interested in this type of position. I had some rock star introverts on my team, but these positions required bold leadership, a willingness to push through unpopular decisions, and the nimbleness to hit the ground running each day with changeable deadlines and priorities. And much of the team was simply there to handle the basics and get a paycheck.

I alerted HR to our challenges and I prayed. After dozens of interviews, we were unable to find a true leader to assist. Ultimately, I needed to groom those who I had or we would all be working 12–14-hour days. After examining the traits and skills within the existing team, I was left with Dan and Harley. Dan was extremely lazy, but would work as long as he was being led and fed. Harley could do her job whenever she would show up.

So, I suggested to Harley that we do some grooming for leadership. If she could get to work at a decent time to meet daily deadlines and quit the gossip, we would be off to a good start to achieve internal equity and set her up to be more respected as a team leader.

Harley responded, "How about you just promote me and give me around $118,000 a year and you can groom me later? I just want my time back for the times that I've worked over."

I was flabbergasted. This was another clue to her internal reality. "The time that you've worked over? You're out more than you are in," I thought to myself.

I told her that wasn't going to work and advised her that I had done the job for a year without a pay increase to prove that I could handle it. "So, let me groom you and we'll discuss an increase later." She was her own worst enemy.

☑

Initially, Harley lived about 45 minutes from the office. Even though we were not clock punchers, I needed staggered start times in order to meet all the timelines before us.

I didn't create schedules—I just wanted to ensure that we had proper coverage to handle issues for our west coast sales organization. That meant we couldn't all come in at 7 am and leave at 3 pm. To have as little impact on the team as possible, I worked with the times that people were already coming in so that I could plan appropriate coverage across time zones. No big deal, right?

I needed to balance the work load and not burn out my technical writers. I tried to make everything as fair as possible to each team member. This was to ensure that each writer had approximately the same amount of content to edit and to meet our deadlines as required by the customer.

Harley normally came in around the 9 am–9:30 window. That was perfectly fine, helping to balance the workload equitably across staggered schedules, and providing west coast coverage. With the 9–9:30 time frame, my only request from Harley was that she make the 9 am team meetings that we held every Tuesday. These meetings were in place before I took over the department, and helped us maintain our workday momentum, being scheduled at a time that seemed to suit everyone's needs around subject matter interviews, authoring, and editing.

When Harley was first hired, she could get to work at 9 am. As time went on, that slipped to 9:30. Her commute time living about

10 miles from me was about 45 minutes, and she struggled. I even helped her plan an easier, alternative route. Later, she moved another 45 minutes farther from the office, with the expected result of later and later arrivals.

Increasingly, she began to miss deadlines. Often, a deadline slip of one to two hours coincided with how late she arrived, indicating that the work scheduled would have been reasonable had she arrived when expected.

☑

During Harley's tenure, she had a child and her struggles intensified. I began receiving an almost daily litany of excuses via email, IM, or voicemail:

- The baby has a rash and I need three vacation days.
- My husband is sick and can't take the baby to daycare.
- The auto insurance adjuster is coming to my house. (Why not the office?)
- I am in line at the courthouse to handle a traffic ticket—sorry I forgot to mention that earlier.
- My internet is out, so I can't work remote, and my road is closed so I can't come in either.
- My husband is dehydrated. (My personal favorite)

Repeatedly, because of Harley's habitual absences and tardiness, I had to realign workload and transfer the burden to others. I even had to reassign writers on-the-fly when Harley was unavailable to meet with reps who traveled from Canada or points west to work with her.

☑

After weeks of preparation time and reminders in team meetings, Performance Reviews were due. Harley advised that she could not meet the Thursday deadline. She had worked remote Monday through Wednesday because her baby had a fever (eliminating drivetime), and complained that she had worked 10+ hours each day. Considering the generous lead time, and how seldom she seemed to put in a full eight hours while in the office, I was not particularly inclined to let it slide.

✓

During this time, she was in and out of Dan's office with gossip for weeks. He then came to tell me and we both were frustrated. I had already advised him on ways to shut it down, and asked him to stop bringing it to my office. I already knew that I was dealing with sabotage.

Harley needed a stern conversation. I explained to her that our departmental foundation was cracked and my team couldn't function. She was shocked. "You think that it's me spreading rumors and being toxic?" she asked. I advised her that everything she said and done had grown legs and walked into my office to inform me, so please stop it.

"Focus more on what's right than what's wrong, please and we will all be okay," I counseled her. "You have the potential to excel, but you are in your own way. You are your own worst enemy."

At this point, she went on to tell me that her husband asked her "Well why is it that you can't get to work on time? Your manager is right."

Why would she share that with me?

I told her that she was unmanageable and uncoachable. I knew that she ignored my emails while sending her own, that she came in even later on the days that I traveled. I found that she was incapable of being led or of leading. I pleaded with her that I needed trustworthy people on my team who did not need a babysitter.

She apologized and said she would try to do better, as tears rolled down her cheeks. Try? At this point I was really beyond all the tears that she had cried.

Leadership isn't gossiping about your manager and other team members. What she exemplified was nowhere near being worthy of $118K. She needed to be flat-out fired.

The very next day, last minute...

She left us in a lurch again with two proposals that had to go out by Friday.

Her email read:

Dionne,

I have almost 4 weeks of vacation time left. I need to take 3 days— meaning I'll be away the rest of this week.

She indicated that her daughter's cough had gotten worse and she needed to take her to the doctor. She added that Nikki had agreed to be her backup. The rookie agreed to this without knowing what she was signing up for, and forgot the fact that she was already backing someone else. There was no way she could do the work of three people. Sadly, this is how her colleague manipulated her.

Again, we were in a lurch trying to accommodate Harley's needs. The rookie learned a tough lesson about what she had signed on for. She went to Dan and asked him to assist her. Dan declined, as she had put herself in that position trying to accommodate Harley and her constant needs.

☑

During the height of the gossip wars, Dan came to advise me that Harley called me a liar.

He reported that Harley said, "If she keeps lying to me, there will be problems." He delivered the message as if the conversation were recent. I discovered later that it had occurred years ago, not long after Harley was hired.

When I spoke to Harley about it, she acknowledged the conversation, but indicated that it was years ago, and she apologized. The source of the problem was that she wanted to take a Green Belt training course and I told her that the course was full. She later found that there were still spaces available.

I asked, "As a professional, why didn't you just come talk to me for an explanation instead of trying to slander me?"

"I guess I should have done that, huh?" Harley replied.

I explained to her that my VP, Rick, had advised that there were only two slots available for our *department* to attend due to our work load and the amount of time that would be required for the Green Belt project. Once the first two people finished the course from our department, I could send two more people. So, yes there were still slots available, but not to our department.

"Oh, I feel stupid," she admitted.

I explained that lying goes against everything that I stand for and there's nothing that important in this company that I need to lie about it.

☑

What bothered me most about Harley was the blatant disrespect she exhibited after I tried to help her. I agreed for her to work remote one day a week; the others sometimes did as well, but they all came into the office the rest of the week. I personally would have ensured that I was on time the other four days to show my gratitude for the accommodation.

Having raised two children while attending college and building my own career, I was well familiar with the challenges parenting can pose. I had tried to be supportive and excited for her during her pregnancy, even planning a surprise baby shower. Still, I expected professionalism when she returned to work. It seemed as if Harley felt that motherhood should come with special privileges.

What I really wanted to say to her was "You are not the first woman to have a baby. Women do that all day, every day and have been for centuries when there was no remote work available. They held jobs, raised kids, stood by their husbands, fixed dinner, went to events after work and more. Get over yourself and get your butt to work." I didn't, of course. It was pointless for me to spend my energy on her.

☑

Again, I advised HR Rhonda of the issue I was having with Harley. The response was that as long as she gets her work done, there's not a lot we can do. I explained my concerns about internal equity, and how many times the team had to pick up the slack when Harley did not accomplish her assigned tasks.

"This isn't fair to the team," I countered. "The rest come in daily like clockwork and often stay late to compensate for her lack of attendance."

Ultimately, I made note of every issue I had with her and every time that I contacted Rhonda. I knew that I would need it one day. I was so frustrated at a lack of support from HR. This was just crazy; there seemed no structure or process in Human Resources whatsoever. It seemed that people could do what they wanted to do without consequences, while I was killing myself for no reason. Was I the only one who could see how critical collaboration was for our team, how working in silos could lead to mistakes that literally could cost us millions?

☑

Following her move, Harley asked if she could work remote at least two days each week. I told her she needed to give me something to work with. "I don't even see you trying to get to the office on time for the four days that you need to be in the office. There's no way I can reward bad behavior, and what you are doing is not exemplary of leadership at all."

Given that she struggled to get into the office before her move, it seemed to me that as an adult, she would realize she had to adjust her schedule accordingly when she chose to move even farther away.

She then confided in Dan, "I don't think that Dionne is going to give me the promotion." Guess how I know this?

I advised her that we needed to move past a leadership role, and she really needed to work on simply getting her life together because it was apparent that it was out of control.

Dan was extremely happy.

☑

I needed some advice from my VP, since I couldn't get any relief from Rhonda other than venting. All HR said was "Tell her she is going to get fired if she doesn't get her s*** together, tell her that." Of course, I modified it, but delivered the message.

This scared Harley for all of 5 minutes; her drawled response was "You gone fire me?"

Exasperated, I told my Vice President that I couldn't take the disrespect and lack of professionalism any more. Harley had just shared with me that she was the hardest-working employee on the team. I had just spoken with her again about missing our weekly team meetings.

Rick responded, "I've been where you are with entry-level employees; you need to do one of two things. Tell them that once the door is closed to the team meeting at 9 am, they can't enter. Or place a note on the door once the meeting has started."

I chose to post the note to ensure clarity, and explained verbally what was driving the new policy, as much as I hated it. Thereafter, I dutifully placed a note on the door, reminding staff not to enter once the meeting had started; I made notes available for their later review.

With the new policy in place, Harley was on time for a couple of meetings before she began to lapse into her old ways. She would then text me from her office around 9:15 to say she'd arrived, seen that the door was closed, and did I want her to come in? I advised her "No, you are setting a horrible example for the team."

What most boggled my mind was that she couldn't seem to conceive of this as a problem, even after several colleagues had asked why she couldn't get to work. They were weary of having to pick up her load.

I reminded Harley that when the team meeting notes were released, she could read them in her leisure and see me with any questions.

Again, I explained to Rick and Rhonda that her work performance was suffering and causing the team to work harder and longer, as well as requiring rework/planning from me. It was too much.

They agreed to draft a PIP. Unfortunately, the plan was delayed, as Rhonda traveled to handle transition when we were acquired by another company. She was out of pocket for about two weeks. My VP was traveling as well, so it was nearly a month before we could meet again to discuss the PIP. During this time Harley already knew that things didn't look good, so she began to look for new opportunities within the company. I was unaware that she was interviewing.

☑

"I can't want it for you; you have to want it for yourself," I had told Harley sadly as we put her PIP in place.

Harley now had major issues with me. I had tried to quell the office gossip. I had asked her to be punctual and professional. I had posted the note on the door during meetings, embarrassing her when she was late. And I had passed her over for promotion and placed her on a PIP. At that point, she began to come in around 11 am and leave at 4 pm. I guess she decided she could work peak hours and count her commute as part of her workday.

I had concluded that Harley could not be coached nor trusted. She had real talent and capability, but she continually derailed her own success.

I had tried to coach her, even taking her to a conference to show her what leadership looks like. Seemingly, staying mired in destructive behaviors was more important than transitioning to leadership and growth.

Nikki

After months of drama with Harley, Debbie, and the rest, the team was exhausted. They were working harder to make up for those whose work performance was slipping, and I was having to do too much rework/planning to keep the momentum going. Our rookie arrived just months before the drama really heated up, and she was the fresh air we needed.

As a millennial, Nikki's emotional intelligence quotient (EQ) was still being nurtured. She was bright, and hard-working, and I looked forward to coaching her to the next level. Nikki and I had a great relationship—we even had our own catchphrase. When we agreed on an issue or topic, our confirmation word was "Gucci." I have a millennial daughter, so I fully understood her lingo.

Sadly, in the midst of the toxic team, Nikki's EQ became compromised. She was fresh blood to the miserable team members. Because of her kind personality and limited experience with workplace politics, she started lending her ear to Downer Debbie. Nikki, not knowing how to draw the line, said "Well that's not my relationship with Dionne." Sadly, over time I could see her personality and attitude begin to shift.

Toxic team members spread through teams and organizations like a horrible disease. Once they learned that she didn't shut down their gossip, she was tainted, leaving her open to the other predators on the team. These colleagues should have served as her role models, helping her to achieve success. Instead, they brought her into their drama, and she wanted to be one of the gang.

For months, Nikki was forthright about her team interactions. I cautioned her about the dangers of office gossip. "I'm only venting my workplace frustrations," she once said to me. I told her it was way more than that, but she didn't understand it then. Later, she was the one who really took things to an entirely different level, after saying to me, "I'll make note of my water cooler conversations and try to stay positive in a busy work season."

✓

In the meantime, VP Rick and I had a meeting with a few executives about the proposal database where we stored our proposal content. The content needed to be refreshed.

I told the executives that I was aware of the need, but also aware of the deadlines that stare us in the face daily. "If this is what needs to be done, I will do my best, but I either need additional resources or we need to cut back on the number of proposals that we respond to. There just aren't enough hours in the day to do it all. But, trust me—I get it."

Rick advised that we need the right people to do the job. If we don't have the right people, then we need to find them. I said ok.

My team was already burned out, but I delivered a sanitized and softened version of Rick's message.

Harley and Nikki were the main database administrators, and this function needed a technical writer to clean up the content. So, I came up with a plan to expedite the library update by having the team participate and send updated content to the two of them.

Harley had difficulty focusing, and didn't follow my instructions, investing her effort in other library content first. Frustrated, she began sharing her complaints with Nikki. Naïve Nikki fell for it. Neither brought their concerns to me.

The secret conversations went back and forth via instant messaging. Then, they made an oopsie. I received this IM from Nikki.

Nikki

It's tough to know what to do about this—is it supposed to be a threat? She says, "I don't intend to scare you—I'm just sharing the word from upper management."

McGee, Dionne

WOWWWW! Guess I'm on your mind.

I was so much on their minds, that the Rookie inadvertently sent the message to me.

Nikki immediately came to my office to apologize, as this was unprofessional. She admitted that she was talking to Harley via IM for days about me. Harley was working remote that day, so I called her via phone in order to speak with both of them.

I explained to them that this was too much and it needed to stop. The sad part was that Nikki and I had a great relationship. Alas, Harley knew that Nikki was naïve enough to fall for her attempts to build an alliance, calling Nikki her little sister. I questioned her, "This is what you would teach your sister?"

The next day I spoke to both of them in my office, Harley first. I reminded her that this was Nikki's first job and this was not what we should be teaching her.

She quickly backpedaled and said that Nikki wasn't talking to her on IM—it must have been someone else. I asked if she was sure, and she said yes. Nikki came in and I asked who she was talking to. Harley tried desperately to stop her from answering, talking over her. The truth was out.

I sent them both a written warning and requested a response of how it could have been handled differently. I received one from Nikki, but not from Harley, who continued to make excuses.

☑

This incident was part of a bigger picture. I'd received notice from colleagues that the team was gossiping about me, particularly when I was out of the office. I wasn't clueless; I'd seen them scattering from various offices when I entered the building, and I'd noted ample evidence of the toxic brew in which my team stewed.

Dionne Griffin McGee

4 THE TOXIC TEAM UNITES

The lion's primary competitor is the hyena, and hyenas outnumber lions 3-1 in the Serengeti. Hyenas travel in clans, and will steal food from the lion's pride when able.

At the end of the day, Harley knew that we were at the end of the road and she had to think quickly to save her job.

Since she knew of issues where team members couldn't get their way, she used that as leverage to form an alliance against me. These are the same people that she came in my office to complain about regularly, but she needed them now.

- She reached out to the one who couldn't get the 6 am–2 pm schedule he wanted.
- She reached out to the one who had a pie job, and was unhappy when asked to do work during work hours.
- She reached out to the one who felt as if he was overlooked for my position.
- She reached out to the rookie, pouring toxic venom into her daily.

Increasingly, I would see some of the team scuttle among their offices, whispering. When I came into the office unexpectedly, I'd find them huddled together. I knew that the alliance was becoming stronger. But my attitude was "I have work to do and HR has been useless at this point." I had too much work to do, too many deals to win.

Shortly thereafter, Harley alerted a colleague that she would be late for that day's team meeting, but did not advise me. She arrived late and disrupted our meeting. I asked if I could speak with her outside, and she agreed. I suggested that we walk down to her office to avoid the ears that I knew were pressed against the wall. I reminded her of our process to avoid disrupting team meetings. I also asked that she notify me directly rather than via her colleagues when she was going to be late.

"Yes ma'am," she replied with a mock military smirk.

She then emailed Tony, our VP of Human Resources with a request to talk.

I know this because Tony emailed Dan while I was meeting with him, and his email popped up on the screen as Dan was projecting a screenshare.

Tony asked "Why is Harley emailing me? What do I need to know?" I saw the email as Dan opened it directly in front of me. I didn't mention it, because I wasn't supposed to see it. But Dan knew that I saw it. Proof of the good-old boys' network. Why not call me?

On the day of Harley's meeting with HR Tony, she arrived in the office with a look straight from goodwill—rumpled clothes, damp, unstyled hair, and a face that looked unwashed. She was in full costume to portray her role as a victim.

One thing a man can't stand is to see a woman cry. Harley was a master at conjuring crocodile tears, playing the victim game—she'd done so with me many times. Tony called me to advise that Harley made some strong accusations against me.

"Really," I replied. "That's what people do when you place them on a PIP."

Tony's response? He advised her to work remote the remainder of that day and the next few days to get herself together. I'm sure she laughed all the way home.

He also advised that he would have his team member, Linda do an investigation to determine what was going on in the department. He noted, "This investigation is confidential, and no one should be discussing this matter at all." I told him that was perfectly fine because I knew all that I had done was my job.

Harley could pull the wool over Tony, but not me and she knew it, which is why she felt it was time to intensify the situation and take another approach. She had just applied for another job and she needed a way out. There's power in numbers, so she needed the team to help her push to this other role and make me look like the bad guy. She invoked the phrase "hostile work environment" and people began to scramble.

HR began conducting interviews, including with me. I requested that they interview the entire team, including contractors and my colleagues. Linda agreed that she would do this, but did not follow through, limiting her interviews to the five toxic team members.

In the meantime, I watched the five collaborate on notes and rehearse what they would say. I watched Harley in Debbie's office, with her typed notes. "That's good, that will work" Debbie proclaimed loudly to alert Harley that I could see them as I rounded the corner towards them. Harley followed with conversations with Dan, Nikki, and Alex, plotting and scheming.

I called Tony to advise him that the team was openly discussing the matter with each other, and his response was "You have to expect that they're gonna talk." I asked what happened to this being confidential with no discussions on the matter. Again, useless.

Soon, I received an invitation to my own interview. I had requested an extended interview. Linda's posture, tone, and facial expressions spoke volumes as we began. Her body language already told me that she believed all that had been said. The interview proceeded more like an interrogation, as if I were a criminal. I answered all her questions and added details where she was misguided.

All my earlier conversations with my HR partner seemed not to matter. It didn't matter that Linda had previously told Dan that Debbie should be gone—and had even commiserated with me that I had to put up with her negativity. I didn't matter that she had written a watered-down PIP for Harley while she was attending to the merger. Wasn't this the same HR rep who had previously said to me, "I heard that you finally got the team in shape. Good for you. I know your role is difficult with all the back-to-back proposals, and with the team you have, I can only imagine."

I spoke candidly with my VP about the situation as it progressed. He assured me that he was pleased, he was proud, and I had nothing to worry about.

"You're a good person and I wouldn't place the department in the hands of anyone else. Don't worry, it will all be fine," he reassured me.

THE VERDICT

The investigation closed on a Monday afternoon. I arrived at the Chief People Officer Tony's office, along with my Vice President, Rick, and the HR Business Partner, Linda, who had spearheaded the investigation.

My VP kicked off the meeting by advising me that we were at the close of the investigation and they had determined that my department was a toxic environment. They indicated that my tone with the team members was more of a dictatorship than a democracy. I had gossip and performance issues among my team members.

He noted, "We didn't find anything that was extreme on your part. However, we suggest that you step aside and transition to another position within the company and continue to report to me or to Tim. It seems that the team has been stressed and that you made [the environment] more stressful.

I leaned forward to clarify. "So, let me get this right. We worked nearly 70 projects last year, which was mandated by my leadership team. I recall telling you there was too much at the gate. And because people can't get their way I need to move to another position?"

"Because Alex can't work 6–2 so he can come in and check the stock market and Facebook? Because the 9 o'clocker comes in at 10 and cries when she can't come and go as she pleases? Because the coordinator can't watch videos all day, message her husband, and do her math homework? Because my Technical Manager really doesn't want my job, but he doesn't want me to have it I need to move? Is that what you're telling me?"

Tony then indicated that Harley and Debbie were leaving the department too. That really confused me. "They are the most toxic people on the team. Since you know that, why move me?"

Rick responded "Once a department becomes a hostile environment, it's hard to start fresh, so we want all of you—including you—to have a fresh start and to be able to excel."

Tony added that the company has a flex-time culture and he'd like to keep that culture. He had heard that people had to be to work at a certain time and he then knew that something had to be done.

So again, I'm confused. Since reporting to Rick, we've increased the amount of proposals that we submit annually by at least 30–40%, increasing from an average of 45 proposals a year to 66 proposals a year. And we have to focus on flex-time? My mind reeled.

I needed someone to tell Rick that. I needed someone to tell the companies that had submitted proposal requests to us with 2–3-week deadlines. I needed to know this when I missed my children's events and family vacation, when I worked on vacation. Flex-time, really? Well how will the job get done if everyone is flexing?

I wish someone had told me that eight years ago when I first started working here with an abusive manager. I worked 12 to 14-hour days weekly in a toxic environment, almost killing myself for this company. Each project has at least thirty milestones before we can complete and submit, and I was managing as many as thirteen simultaneously. And I have to wonder where my team members are while they are free to come and go as they please?

"I need to be able to balance resources so that we don't get burned out. If you are looking for that manager where people can come and go as they please and to still be able meet all these deadlines…then I am definitely not the manager you are looking for," I said.

I thought back to the early years of my tenure. I had vowed that I would work my way to a leadership role so that we wouldn't have to work 12–14-hour days. Once I made it to leadership, I knew that resource leveling was essential in order to keep our workdays reasonable and our workload fair across the team. This would require some of the lazy people who weren't pulling their weight to step up.

I shifted in my seat and looked at each representative.

"I want to make sure that I am clear. You interviewed five toxic people who didn't like me from the gate because they couldn't get their way. I've been here for eight years, giving you blood, sweat, and tears, and this is how you show your appreciation."

I followed with questions:
- Did you interview my other team members and contractors as I requested? NO
- Did you interview my colleagues as I requested? NO
- Did you interview any of the other 80-plus employees that I work with on a daily basis? NO

- Did you interview third-party customers that I work with? NO
- Does my work performance over the years reflect that I am a bully? NO
- Rick, have you ever had any issues or concerns with me or my performance? NO

Am I direct? Yes, but I'm no one's bully. The environment became hostile because they created it, and HR did absolutely nothing to support me. Let's come to work and get the job done and leave the drama at home. That's all I asked. But every step of the way the team wanted to undermine every decision I made. I can honestly say on some level I understand how President Obama must have felt.

I continued, "You laid off our former female manager for similar concerns, and she and I are nothing alike. So, you thought you rectified the situation when you merely got rid of part of the problem. But you left me with the remnants of a toxic team to lead. You set me up for failure every step of the way. Did you ever consider that?"

"I'll own that," Tony replied. "I guess we all could have done a lot of things differently."

I looked at him. "The job is overwhelming and it can't be done with toxic people. The fact is that they have severely exaggerated truths, that they've flat-out lied, cried, and collaborated on this performance. I watched them whisper and run from office to office to conspire on what they would say."

"But you want me to step aside? It's clear to me that you've made up your mind and I'm wasting my breath. So, what's the offer on the table?"

Rick responded, "Because of who you are and all that you've done for the company, the dedication and drive that you have shown in leading us to multi-million-dollar wins, we think this is best. Take a few days off to clear your mind. I'll come by your office to chat."

I felt strangely buoyant as I left the meeting and went back to my office. Rick arrived soon after and closed the door. "I know that you've saved my a** more times than I can mention getting the bids out the door."

I'm thinking to myself, "Why didn't you say all of that with the Chief People Officer? Why didn't you say 'I know I placed you under major duress to get the job done' in front of the others?"

5 THE LONELY WALK

Lions do much of their hunting in the dark hours between dusk and dawn. While the females do most of the hunting, male lions patrol the territory and protect the pride.

As I've stated on numerous occasions, leadership is a lonely walk. As long as you want to be average, people are okay, but when you want to excel you become a target. I wanted more. I wanted excellence. I wanted to lead others to be their best selves, to encourage and coach them to reach their own dreams.

Do I have any regrets? Not a one. Can I say that I made major strides and changes in the department? Yes, I can. In fact, I left the department on the heels of a $195 million win. And with a decidedly better project management approach.

I refused to dim my light so that others could be comfortable. I know who I am, I know to whom I belong, and I knew that this was the segue to something far more meaningful than I could have ever dreamed or imagined.

It's None of My Business
A wise person once said "It's none of my business what others say about me." I agree wholeheartedly. People will talk, regardless of if they feel that you are right or wrong. Sometimes individuals will simply be pissed when change is on the horizon, when structure is in place, when efficiency matters.

I have to answer to a higher power, and as long as God is pleased with my decisions, the decisions that I've discussed with Him, then I feel good about them. As a woman of integrity and accountability, I had found it very difficult to work on a dysfunctional team. I quickly realized that my values, principals, and beliefs were different than those of many of my team members. No one had to look for me or ask if I was at work, because I was where I was supposed to be, doing what I was hired to do and more. I was dedicated to the cause.

What was my purpose or agenda in doing so? I was there to represent every African-American little girl in elementary school, junior high, high school, and college. I represented those females who haven't even decided yet that they will work in the energy arena.

I was the only African-American female in leadership within the company. Not only was my team 100% Caucasian—so were my peers and the majority of the other 4000-plus people in the company. This situation was sometimes difficult, but my vision was bigger, and I enjoyed the company and my colleagues. I was there because I was paving the way of leadership for those who will come after me, those whom I may never meet. This is the legacy that I need to show my children and all others.

During those dark days, I often pondered my purpose there.

I knew that I could change lives for the better, but were these the lives that I was supposed to be changing?

I couldn't see it. I then realized that this part of the journey was to change my life. Through this metamorphosis, I had refused to let my light dim to make others comfortable. At times, I felt bad for them, because they had no idea of who I was and how much I wanted to help them.

No, this was not the type of team I had planned to manage or lead. It was not what I wanted, but I am not a quitter. That would have been too easy. And it would've played into their hands.

I began to understand that what I was experiencing wasn't just about me. If I was dealing with these challenges, so were others. Out of that realization, this book came to be. It was my service to others and therapy for myself without the copay.

People will not always celebrate you, and that's okay. Ultimately, I decided that I need not waste any more energy on the people who brought me negative energy, but to focus on those who were in the office to excel in their careers and who brought positive energy into the workplace.

I had internal equity at stake, and I had to shift from the negative energy and let my light shine within the positive energy that already existed.

THE TRANSITION

Back in my office following the HR investigation, Rick said, "Let's plan to talk to the team on Tuesday to make an announcement. You probably don't want to be there, do you?"

"Of course I do! Why wouldn't I? I have no ill will, malice, or retaliation towards any of them. I have zero regrets about holding them accountable. I am good and want to say my goodbyes and wish them well in their future endeavors," I responded.

The meeting was planned for Tuesday, following my time off to "clear my head." Then, to my surprise, one of my managers sent an invitation on Rick's behalf for a team meeting on Friday. This was one of the days that I'd been advised to take off, and no one had notified me of the date change. I emailed Rick to tell him that I still planned to attend as I did receive the invitation (probably by mistake). I followed that with the question, "What is my new role?" No email response came.

Rick finally contacted me via phone so I arrived early and we had a meeting in my office. He asked how I was feeling and I simply advised him that I felt betrayed and that injustice had been served. I expressed my regret that as hard and long as I'd worked in the department, this was the thanks I got. But I had to be removed in order to get to where I really needed to be.

✓

I attended the team meeting that day with parting gifts for all of my haters. It was so biblical. I sat at the table in the presence of my enemies. I had previously ordered leather journals for the team and they had arrived just before the meeting. HR and Rick advised the team to think about how they had contributed to the departmental issues and how this could have gone differently.

I then spoke to all of them and stated simply "You have to do this job with the right people, who are passionate about the job. Unfortunately, we don't mesh well at all. I'm passionate about my role and some consider it a job. I will see you all around and I wish you nothing but success in your careers. I've also brought you all parting gifts—every time you use them, think about me." I left the meeting for them to discuss the next steps.

HR moved me to the corporate floor away from the proposal team. But Rick and I had already discussed that I would work primarily remote. It didn't make sense that my entire organization was all over the country and worked remote, but that I would have to come in the office just because I was located in the same city as headquarters.

Days later, they let my VP go. We were at a going-away party for our current president and Rick asked if he could chat with me. "Sure," I responded.

"Are you ready for the other shoe to drop?" he asked.

"Aww crap, what now?" I responded.

"I'm leaving," Rick said, simply.

"Are you kidding?" I exclaimed.

"No," and I knew that he was serious by the look on his face. He looked disgusted. He then began to relate to me, "I know for a fact that there is no way that we could have accomplished all that we have together had you not led the department. We were a great team, you and me. I hope that you would still reach out to me and feel free to still consider me as your coach/mentor. Again, I apologize for not hearing you."

My eyes swelled with tears.

NEW ROLE

I transitioned into my new role as Senior Manager of Sales Operations. When I tell you that I am so happy… I don't even have the words. God is good. My stress level has decreased by 200%. No toxic team members, no attitudes and sour dispositions, no constant daily deadlines. My work ethic was entirely too strong for people who wanted to show up and hang out at work and not get the job done. It was definitely time to move on and continue to work with the professional sales organization and let the team find their own way. You can't coach people who don't want it.

At the same time, I continued to perfect my professional speaking skills and speaking to audiences at every opportunity. The feedback was enormously positive, and I gave my all to coaching every client who needed my guidance. The personal rewards were so gratifying. This is how I knew I was doing the right thing. You just have to do the right thing with the right people and you will know that you have purpose.

✓

I flew into Nashville to present at one of our corporate sales meetings. While in Nashville, my new manager and I had planned to go over my performance evaluation for the year.

I met Tim for my review, which was stellar, as usual. He had interviewed my peers, as well as included his own experience with me—and noted that folks were glad to have me remain a part of the sales organization. I asked Tim what my performance rating was—Exceeds Expectations, Meets Expectations? He said that he didn't have a ranking at that time, but HR had advised that they would take into consideration the things that went on in the proposal department. I said that's fine. I wasn't worried, because I knew that I did my job.

I knew too that I had gone above and beyond both that year and every year since I'd been there. For eight years running, I had been dedicated to the cause, skipping lunch, working from home, missing children's events and family trips. I had missed out on life for eight years because I let my career consume me. So, because of the drama, I might possibly get a Meets and not an Exceeds rating this year.

Tim and I chatted on where the role was going and that I had nothing but success in front of me. He confided, "I really don't know what happened in the past, but you are in a place now where we support your success, so let's forget that and move on."

I delivered my presentation at the sales meeting to a warm reception. Sales meetings continued into the next day, and I was scheduled to return home Friday, when incentive pay was to be distributed. I checked my bank account and saw that there was no deposit. I contacted the HR department of the company that had recently acquired us, as Sally was our new HR representative.

Sally said, "Let me find out what's going on, Dionne, and I'll call you back." In the meantime, I contacted my manager Tim as well. He began to investigate and contacted our original HR staff.

Later that afternoon, Sally called back to say, "Dionne, let me profusely apologize to you, before I say this. This is not how we should be handling business, but unfortunately when you're a Below Expectations, you don't qualify for an incentive."

I was stunned. "Please forgive me Sally, but did you just say Below Expectations?"

"Yes, I apologize that you had to find out this way."

"So am I, Sally. So am I!"

My mind returned to the recent efforts I had made to pull things together for the largest deal that the company had ever won, to the miracle I'd helped bring about to save the deal when my team member purposely dropped the ball to sabotage me. Remember his comment "If any of this s*** falls through the cracks, it all falls on you." I'd just gotten an outstanding performance review earlier in the week, and I was Below Expectations?

It didn't seem possible, but I knew exactly how it could happen. So, I relate this story with clarity of thought, mind, and deed. The issues that strong, African-American females face in the world are the same in corporate America. Just because we are strong, vocal, educated and passionate doesn't make us angry, heartless, or inconsiderate. It makes us wake up to win on a daily basis.

ETHICS AND COMPLIANCE

I contacted Jason at our newly acquiring company's Chief Ethics and Compliance Office. Jason listened attentively and asked if I felt that they put too much weight on the issues in the department.

"No," I responded. "My concerns are that they put all the weight on something that is not true. But HR wouldn't listen. People don't resist change; they resist being changed. I held them accountable. Come to work and let's work and leave the negative energy at home."

Jason contacted Tony from our original HR team, and Tony advised him that this was a delicate issue and it was best that the local HR staff talk to me. In a couple of days, I heard not from Tony, but from Ham, his subordinate. Ham and I scheduled a meeting.

I was faintly surprised that Tony was not meeting with me personally, until I remembered him saying once "Management wouldn't be so bad if people weren't involved."

I met with Ham, but it seemed clear that he was going through the motions because Tony had sent him. I could just feel his bias. I explained to him all the steps that I had taken to handle our departmental issues, and the only thing I felt that I could have done differently was to have gone to Tony directly. In fact, I had gone to Tony on two occasions only to find sticky notes on the door, where he was traveling for weeks at a time.

Ham probably felt that I requested the meeting for the incentive bonus. That wasn't the case. I requested the meeting because I smelled a rat. I've never had a BE performance rating in my entire career. I continued, "You listened to five toxic gossipers who couldn't get their way. I'd dared to say, 'No, you can't show up when you want to. No, you can't come in early because you are senior and like to get up early. No, you can't leave when you want to, no you can't do your homework at work, no you can't play Candy Crush all day and hang out on Facebook.'"

"Moreover, you want to rate me a BE, and I have yet to see it in writing anywhere; it was all verbal. If I was truly a BE, then I should be placed on a PIP so that I can be aware of what I need to work on. But you can't put it into writing because you know there's nothing to write—because it's bogus." Ham proceeded to tell me that the proposal group was doing well now. "And don't fret, the BE won't be noted or recorded anywhere." (Are you starting to smell that rat now?)

"I bet they are, because all eyes are on them now. They have to get the job done."

He went on, "Harley seems to be doing fine."

"So you think," I told him. I related that I was aware that she had only one vacation day remaining when she left the team. And yet, she had lied to her new manager and took two weeks of vacation at the Christmas holiday because she didn't have anyone to hold her accountable.

"But you want to question my integrity? How dare you?"

The look on his face was priceless. The old HR department didn't have anything in place to track vacation details until the new company came along. They ran a mom and pop operation. On the other hand, I had kept thorough records for my team.

Essentially, I relayed that they had been played. "What happened to talking to me?" I asked. "Even a murderer knows the charges that are held against them."

"No, I'm not here about the money," I told him squarely. "I'm here because I'm not a BE and never have been. My ask is that you be fair. You listened to five people." I continued:

- What about my (5) peers that I've worked with for eight years?
- What about the (30) employees that report to them?
- What about the (30-plus) people on the water team?
- What about the (15) people who are in the marketing department?

I concluded, "I see what's going on here and I will rectify the situation. If I had to deal with this, then that means that I'm not the only one. However, I am strong enough to bring light to the situation because it's wrong, dead wrong."

Ham and I scheduled a follow-up meeting and I sent him my notes, which I also shared with my former HR business partner, who did not review them. In our second meeting, Ham mentioned that he did not know all the details of my case, and I had to wonder if I was wasting my time. He went on to say "You are pointing the finger at everyone else. Maybe you should look at yourself."

I said, "You know what, Ham? I already did, and I already told you what I could have done differently. However, I appreciate your time," and I stood to leave. This had been a complete waste of time.

In speaking with my new manager Tim later, he observed, "Something is fishy." During his own investigation, he had asked many of the same questions I had, and learned that HR did not talk to peers or look at past performance reviews. Nor had they talked to others in the company who work with me daily.

Tim got it. He's had a toxic team before and he knows what it feels like. He said "I'd rather be a team of one than to have one toxic person on the team." I totally agreed.

I told Tim that since the HR team had not been what I needed them to be, I'd like to talk to Matt the VP and Mick the new company president. "You do whatever you need to do to clear your mind. But just know you're in a position now where we support you and your growth. Just don't let this consume you."

I did speak with our new President, Mick. HR had not shared details with him, so I recapped for him, outlining the team makeup, the investigation, and the outcome with HR. Mick began to nod and ask questions.

I told him that the whole situation was absurd. How do we have an HR Department that's not available when you need them and doesn't talk to the employees? Especially one in leadership? Just because five people said it doesn't make it true. Did anyone check their motives? Absolutely not. They were all PIP-worthy, but since they said it and HR gave me the opportunity for leadership, they seemed to think "We met our quota so let's do something different." I continued, "Our diversity and inclusion numbers always looked horrible; I bet they didn't change that for the only female African-American in leadership. I can guarantee it." I painted the picture for Mick and he had an ah-ha moment.

He then wanted to know my ask. I simply told him that all I wanted was for this to NEVER happen to another employee. I added that HR needs investigation skills, listening skills (not talking—listening), they need to not be biased or discriminatory. It's not about the incentive because they had no idea that building wealth was the least of my worries. My issue is I can't stand injustice and I won't tolerate it from anyone. They didn't want to listen, but if I have encountered this, so has someone else.

Mick agreed that all I was asking was fair.

He and Tim were the only people who really heard me and understood what I tried to tell so many. He allowed me his unbiased, non-judgmental ear. He thanked me for setting up the meeting and educating him on my HR experience.

(What's baffling to me is that corporations now have to make a mental note to create diversity and inclusion teams. Really, just do the right thing and a team isn't needed. But, pay close attention to who sits on these diversity teams. Is it really diverse?)

Following my meeting with Mick, we encountered HR Linda in the hallway. I spoke, but she merely smirked and turned away. That response told me that Ham had shared our earlier conversation with her. I had to wonder why she was so angry.

In reality, I had made too many people uncomfortable. I had refused to accept mediocrity from myself or my team, from HR or my own managers. I never would step aside—only step up. It was clear that I needed to step up to the injustice happening around me.

And so, I began to write my truth.

✓

Not long after I left the proposal department, I received a call from a possible new hire that she was in the lobby waiting to interview with me. I advised her that she must be looking for Dan. This probably occurred because the internal contract agency had not been updated that I was no longer leading that department.

They finally hired a new proposal manager externally. Ironically, the company ended up overlooking Dan once again and hiring a new manager. Dan had tons to learn about leadership, a healthy work environment, and helping build a strong team—not being one of the culprits who attempts to take it down.

Dionne Griffin McGee

AFTERWARD

New levels bring new devils. I was built for the drama. While I was still with the proposal team, I thanked God for trusting me with trouble on a daily basis. In the beginning, I didn't understand it, but I began to understand that He was preparing me for something more. I know that I am not the only one who has struggled with sabotage in a leadership position.

As an African-American female in a male-dominated industry, I know the struggle is real. I am weary of the daily battle just to make it. It's simply too much to do alone. We must encourage one another, just as the strong women in my life encouraged me and each other. I want to help others, especially women, move past these struggles—it's become an integral part of my life's purpose. In the words of Lisa C. at one of my conferences, "There's a special place in hell for women that don't help other women."

New Jersey Lieutenant Governor Sheila Oliver nailed it when she observed, "We often talk about shattering the glass ceiling. When I hear someone say, 'Yes, some of us have crashed through the glass ceiling,' [I think] but there are still a lot of women down in the basement, sweeping up the glass."

Following the experiences that I had, I vowed to live my life to the fullest from this day forward and to help free others from similar injustice. Within my own company, I didn't want those who came behind me to encounter what I did. More than that, I wanted to empower others. My experiences gave birth to this book.

WHAT SUCCESS LOOKS LIKE

I have come to realize that success looks like different things to different people. I now understand that what I thought I wanted, I still want, but the level of intensity is different. Yes, we all want to succeed at life and make it to the top. It is challenging to lead people who don't want to be led. It is hopeless to push people who don't want to go anywhere.

In defining success for myself, I had always thought of amazing Christian connection, the nice home, nice cars, being debt-free, having a great marriage, enjoying good health, having my children doing well, and my parents possessing good health. I wanted work that was challenging, gratifying, and fulfilling.

As I've learned, not everyone wants this. Some just want the 9 to 5. Let me come in and do some work, watch videos, play video games, check the stock market, gossip at the water cooler, smoke cigarettes, eat lunch, and go home. They want to do as little as possible to get a paycheck. That's not who I am. And I simply dislike lazy people.

Three months before I exited the proposal department, I asked God to fix my situation. I knew that I could not sustain the pace I was keeping, nor with the people on the team. I had reasoned with my team. I had talked to HR countless times without results. I had worked so hard to give the team some balance in their own work lives, but I had none in my own. It was time for a change. I had to pray.

I did a great deal of self-examination. Was it me? Was I the one with the issues? I looked at all my relationships within the company all the way up to the president, and my relationships outside my team were solid.

I looked at my family, my church family, and my friends. We all had great relationships. I asked my corporate mentor, Willette, if it was me. She said "No, you just have some lazy people on your team who don't want to support you, and that's sad. Too bad Human Resources hasn't been any support either."

My environment didn't want me to be great, but thank God I was fully aware of who I was. Leaders build other leaders, but these people were not aware of who they were or whose they were.

So, I prayed. And God began to reveal some things to me. Success was not about the house, and the cars, especially if I had to be under so much stress to have them. Was it really worth it? Now I understand why so many people turn down promotions and reject a move to the top. Success is different for so many people.

Following the HR investigation, my role changed. I agreed to the change and thanked God. The experience had been so painful. Did I like the way that He answered my prayer? Not at first, but I then remembered what I had asked for. Success is different as I look through a new pair of lenses. In my new role I can really work eight-hour days. I've got my life back.

With that time, my life has changed for the better.

- My relationship with Christ has grown and I'm more involved in my church.
- I'm able to make all of our family events.
- I can make my son's school and sporting events.
- My stress level has decreased markedly.
- I'm able to cook healthy meals.
- I'm able to take walks and exercise regularly with my husband.
- I'm able to visit my parents and family more.
- I have fewer doctor's appointments.
- I've lost 25 pounds. Actually, I've lost around 900 pounds of toxic people.

Final Thoughts
Women want to be heard when we speak, just like the next person at the boardroom table. **Time out for women being afraid to**

speak up and not being heard! Our ideas are just as good if not better than our male counterparts. We need our male leaders to understand that we bring value and are remarkable assets to any company or organization that's blessed to have us.

We also need our male leaders—Directors, Vice Presidents, and Presidents—to understand the emotional intelligence required when having a woman in leadership, especially an African-American woman in leadership. Many won't like her just because the sky is blue. Female leaders know that we have to work harder and longer to prove ourselves as we continue to face the gender wage gap. Today, on average, a woman earns **80.5 cents** for every dollar a man earns, and women's median annual earnings are $10,086 less than men's, according to data from the US Census Bureau.

I've been fortunate enough to coach a number of women on how to find their inner lion—the lion in the jungle of course. This was the real success. The ability to pour into the lives of others is more rewarding than I could have ever imagined. It has opened the door to speak across the country and to address the issues that women face in corporate America. I know far too many women who have experienced the same struggle.

That struggle is epidemic—we are simply not being heard. In the boardroom and sometimes in marriage, women are losing the very essence of their being. Some aren't heard in church, and some feel as if life is just passing them by. We are tired of being known only as our spouse's wives and our childrens' mom; we too have a life to live.

I am well aware that some of us have signed up to be stay-at-home moms, and that's perfectly fine. I totally get it. Especially in this crazy world, it can be safer and more economical to stay home with our children. One could easily spend her salary on childcare, so it makes sense. There isn't a salary yet negotiated for being a mom. It's simply priceless. However, some women thrive as individual contributors, leaders, and entrepreneurs.

And despite how amazing we are, we as women tend to shy away from applying for positions if we feel that we don't meet all the requisition requirements. How about our male counterparts sometimes not meeting any of the requirements and getting the job? We must be the lion in the jungle and go and get everything to which we are entitled. So what? You don't meet all the requirements. Stop waiting for someone to acknowledge your skills and say "You know there's a position open; I think you should apply." We need to acknowledge what we bring to the table and take that leap!

Only two things can happen. We get the opportunity or we don't. If we get it, great. If not, we still win. We should simply ask for a follow-up as to why, so that we can grow from it. Maybe it's a skill that was missing, a class that was needed, or a certification. That's how we win; take the leap, get the information, and just jump.

We must find our inner lion. Until we are all able to let our voices be heard, I will continue to be a voice of the woman. I will stand at the mountaintop and roar until we can all roar together. There IS power in numbers! I am a lion in the jungle, in spite of others' attempts to sabotage my character, my integrity, and my career. I always persevere, and I strive to help others who seek personal or professional development. When you work in a capacity of excellence to go above and beyond, you can't have people on your team who work in a capacity of mediocrity. The two just won't mesh.

I see the struggle daily. Racism, ageism, gender bias, lack of mentors or sponsors, no work-life balance, and unconscious bias—all are real issues that people deal with daily in the workplace. But as poet Nikki Giovanni asserts, "**Deal with yourself as an individual worthy of respect and make everyone else deal with you the same way.**"

We can roar—I've seen the results. My sales and marketing experience have allowed me to become the visionary behind one of the fastest-growing direct sales jewelry brands. I've been able to purchase investment property. My family and I have built a phenomenal team of go-getters, and we are grateful. I share this to say that you don't have to be limited to work in corporate life. You can create your own corporation. This is what leaders do! We create other leaders.

No weapon formed against me shall prosper. I'm reminded of a dream that I had a while ago. I've known for some time that I was supposed to impact lives and alter legacies. I knew that I was supposed to speak, and I did so at a leisurely pace.

Then, one night I fell asleep and found myself at the gates of heaven. A long line of people waited, trying to get into heaven. I was ecstatic as I stood outside the pearly gates. It was too much to take in. Heaven is glorious, just as the Bible says. I saw streets paved with gold, choirs signing—all simply bright and glorious. Everyone was smiling, with no worries, no cares or fears.

I began peeking between the gates to see if I could glimpse any family members. When I finally made it to the front of the line, I told God, "God, I am honored to stand in your presence. I stand in awe of your glory. I thank you for keeping me from dangers seen and unseen. I thank you for dying on the cross for me. I thank you for protecting me and my family all these years."

He simply said, "You're welcome daughter, so glad that you made it up. You've done well and I am pleased. Let me get your chart. Stay here; I'll be right back." He returned with my chart and said, "You've overcome some challenges and you've done well. Everything looks good here, but I have just one concern."

I said, "Oh my father. What could that be?"

He responded, "I called, created, and equipped you to speak and impact lives, and I don't see where you did what I created you to do. Can you please explain to me why you didn't do what I called you to do?"

My heart began to hammer, and I broke into a cold sweat. Can you imagine trying to explain to God why you didn't do what he created you to do? Tears began to fall from my eyes.

He related, "Because you didn't do what I created you to do, the goals, dream, ideas and aspirations of others will never be fulfilled, because they never had the opportunity to hear you speak."

I began to apologize profusely for not fulfilling the gift. I woke from the realest dream of my life, bathed in sweat and weeping. I sat up in my bed and asked God to please forgive me and to give me another chance to get it right. Days later, I was invited to speak at a Women in Leadership Conference. I acknowledged, "Okay God, this is the test. I see you." Of course, I accepted. I had no idea who was coming—it didn't matter. I set flight to Boston to speak to 450 women who flew in from across the country.

Just before I was scheduled to speak, I went to the restroom to gather myself and prepare. I said, "Okay God, so we're gonna do it big, huh? I know that this is all you. I ask that you show up and out so that I can impact the lives of everyone in the room."

Soon, I was making what I call the walk of death from my seat to the stage, heart racing. BUT! When I hit the stage, game on. Something rose in me that I can't begin to explain. As I wrapped up my talk, people began to rise in a standing ovation. The event planner hugged me, and the look that she gave me was priceless. One of the staff from the event then sent an email back to my VP proclaiming "A Star Is Born." Unbeknownst to me, the email would go viral. As I retook my seat, tears began to flow from my face, as I remembered my dream. However, those around me didn't know about my dream, and I tried to catch the tears so they wouldn't think I was crazy, but there were just too many. I wanted to scream in celebration, but I could only clap softly as I sat on the front row.

The moment took me back to the movie "The Pursuit of Happyness," starring Will Smith, who portrayed the life of Chris Gardner. Once he was in his element and became the broker that he desired to be through all his struggles and setbacks. He couldn't speak; all he could do was let the tears fall and clap because he had finally found that happiness. I occupied that same moment.

"Thank you for the confirmation, Lord," I prayed. "It's time." That was the day that I found my roar.

Still, I had no idea that my experience would turn into a book and that this book would thrust me into my purposed position even more. This is why I say that all things happen for the good of those who love the lord. The shift is here!

You can accomplish your dreams, goals, and ideas, and not kill yourself to do it. Some would have thought my changing of executive roles bothered me. Honestly, it was the best thing that could have happened to me. The funny part is that God used my haters to put me exactly where I needed to be.

Don't feel sorry for me. I've redefined success and it looks good on me! It troubles me that this is not the case for too many people. Let's connect so that your voice can be heard too.

God gave me everything I wanted and then some. I am now living a truly successful life and so can you! I now understand why I had to go through this test. It wasn't for me. It was so that we could connect. He simply said, "You must tell this story to others, as you are not the only lion dealing with this epidemic. Roar!"

God Bless You!

Dionne

(If you don't remember my name, I pray that you remember His name.).

DISCUSSION QUESTIONS

1. What does leadership look like?

2. Do you have leadership core values and principles?

3. Do you have the right attitude to be a leader?

4. What you believe determines how far you go as a leader. What's your perception of yourself?

5. What do you have to offer?

6. Do you have to be the most intelligent person in the organization, team, church, school, or your circle?

7. Communication skills (Speaking/Listening). How effective are you?

8. Are you equipped to handle racism, sabotage, ageism, and biases? Why do people try to sabotage others?

9. Are you equipped to walk the lonely walk of leadership?

10. List ways that you value your time?

11. Why are there toxic people on your team? (Multiple choice)

a. Inherited them
b. Enabled them
c. Hired them
d. You are them
e. All of the above

12. How should you handle the toxic people in your life, team, church, school?

13. Why does mediocrity make leaders feel uncomfortable?

14. Leaders motivate, empower, and inspire others to be great. Explain how you are doing this.

15. Do you need a mentor or coach? If so, explain why you think so.

16. Are you mentoring or coaching others? How has this helped them and you?

17. What does your altitude plan look like?

18. What steps are you taking to get there?

19. What skills, products, or services do you have to offer the world?

20. List at least 3 ways you can serve the world with your gift in the next 90 days.

ABOUT THE AUTHOR

Empowerment speaker. Change agent. Thought guru. Dionne Griffin McGee brings her insane energy and compelling empathy for women in leadership to her writing, speaking, and coaching roles. Her career, built on over 20 years of corporate life, has included over a decade in the executive suite. What she's learned there has been by turns painful and powerful.

With a special heart for women in the workplace, Dionne has become a powerful advocate for diversity and inclusion. Today, she's using her unique talents to help other budding leaders find their best selves, gain new courage, and embrace their dreams. With a solid foundation in excellence, ethics, and entrepreneurship, her approach resonates with those seeking to find their places in leadership.

Today, Dionne is recognized as a powerful motivational speaker, coach, consultant and now—author. She has had the good fortune to travel the country to inspire thousands to chase after their dreams and goals and not settle for the status quo. "We must be fulfilled; otherwise what's the point of being here? We should live life to the fullest, not just exist. Our voices must be heard in order for us to leave a legacy."

Among her audiences have been Dress for Success, Women in Leadership conferences, Dave Ramsey audiences, sales organizations, churches, non-profits, and more.

Dionne's audiences are energized and engaged by her approachable, dynamic style, sharing comments like:

> *Best speaker of the conference – Monica S., Nashville, TN*
>
> *Amazing speaker – Gloria P, New York, NY*
>
> *Dynamic and inspirational – Allison A, Raleigh, NC*
>
> *So relatable – Danielle A., Boston, MA*
>
> *Great presence – Dawn S, Long Island, NY*
>
> *Loved her!! – Shelly C, Chicago, IL*

Dionne earned her Bachelor's degree from NC Wesleyan College.

Connect with Dionne

Contact the business office at DG McGee Enterprises, LLC at:

PO Box 2293
Garner, NC 27529

Email us at:

info@dgmcgee.com
melody@dgmcgee.com

Visit us at:

www.DGMcGee.com

LinkedIn: linkedin.com/in/dionnegmcgee/

Facebook: DG McGee Motivates

Instagram: DG McGee Motivates

Twitter: @DGMcGeeMotivates

YouTube: DG McGee Motivates

Check out DG McGee Motivates conference services:

- Keynotes
- Coaching
- Consulting
- Workshops/Breakout sessions
- Half-day trainings
- World-class emceeing/moderating

If you are looking for your audience to be impacted and pushed to take a leap, book Dionne today via www.DGMcGee.com!!!

Dionne Griffin McGee

Made in the USA
Columbia, SC
28 March 2019